TWO
SHALL BECOME
ONE

Basic Tips on the Road towards a Successful Relationship

ALSON B. H. PERCIVAL, Ph.D

authorHOUSE®

AuthorHouse™
1663 Liberty Drive
Bloomington, IN 47403
www.authorhouse.com
Phone: 833-262-8899

Published by AuthorHouse 08/11/2021

ISBN: 978-1-6655-3434-5 (sc)
ISBN: 978-1-6655-3433-8 (e)

ACKNOWLEDGEMENTS

I am pleased to express special gratitude to
    VANESSA RAWLINS
        who is responsible for the typing and layout of the material.

To my Administrative Assistant,
    JANETTE RAWLINS
        who gave technical support.

To my friends and colleagues:
    MASTER PEARLETTA LANNS
    HANZEL AND ANNETTE MANNERS
    VENERABLE VALENTINE HODGE
    WENDELL HUGGINS
    HON. MARJORIE MORTON
    Imogen Jones-Morton

AND NATASHA PERCIVAL-RAWLINS

your contributions were invaluable!

PRAYER

O God of Love, To thee we bow,
And pray for these before thee now;
That closely knit in holy vow;
They may in thee be one.
When days are filled with pure delight;
When paths are plain and skies are bright;
Walking by faith and not by sight;
May they in thee be one.
When stormy winds fulfill thy will;
And all their good seems turn to ill;
Then, trusting thee completely still;
May they in thee be one.
Whate'er in life shall be their share.
Of quickening joy or burning care;
In power to do and grace to bear;
May they in thee be one.
Eternal love, with them abide,
In thee forever may they hide,
For even death cannot divide
Those whom thou makest one.

W. Vaugh Jenkins
1868-1920

MARRIAGE IS THE GREATEST HAPPINESS OF ALL

In a marriage,
two people become as one,
yet they are individuals,
each with their own ideas and goals.
In a marriage,
two people share their thoughts.
They give advice,
sharing their feelings,
being open and loving.

(Michelle Gallagher)

FOREWORD

In "The Two Shall Become One" the Venerable Alson B. H. Percival presents valuable information from his experience as a Parish Priest to those who are considering marriage and also for those who are already man and wife. Whether you have been married for many years or are just about to do so you will find advice that applies to your own situation or general principles which you can adapt to your particular context.

As a priest, Archdeacon Percival has based his writing on his Christian faith. As you read through this book you will observe his own trend of thought and theological reflections and views on Marriage, relationships and family life. There are several references to Holy Scripture which you will find to be helpful once you prayerfully reflect on them, and let them be guiding principles throughout your life.

This book is quite simple in its presentation and should be easy reading for all no matter your state in life. You may not agree with everything contained in this book, whether you do or not the important thing is that it is intended to provoke discussion, to help you to reflect, meditate, and seriously consider the sacrament of Holy Matrimony. Hopefully, this will enable you to acquire a mature understanding, and put you in a better position to determine whether you are ready or prepared to enter into this holy union, and to have Christ at the center of your life together.

I commend this book especially to those who are in a relationship and are considering marriage. Read it and have some discussion before you make that important decision.

The Rt. Rev'd C. Leopold Friday.
Bishop of The Windward Islands

AUTHOR'S NOTE

This Book is For Growth in All Relationships

Before you read: You should pray quietly and invite the Holy Spirit to breathe upon your understanding and make you comfortable. At the end of your study, thank the Holy Spirit for His leading in the exercise; and too, remember any who came to mind while you have been impacted with new direction for the better.

Read: Open the book and find the relevant section that will speak vividly to you as per direction. Read slowly and think through the meaning revealed. You may need to reread for clarity.

Section: Each section was specially thought out and researched with a view of helping Christians to fulfil their dreams and aspirations in their chosen relationships.

On Your Journey: You will need to depend on the Holy Spirit's on a daily basis.

Focus: To maintain a focused relationship you and your partner, spouse or friend must connect your life of prayer with God in daily devotion. Any relationship that is before God is sustained only by His daily visitation.

Suggested Prayer: God, who wonderfully saved us and calls us on this new day to continue this earthly journey, seal us afresh by Your Same Holy Spirit as we together fulfil your purpose. Amen

Communication: Trust that this book will excite you and generate your continual interest to pass it on to help others. My passionate hope is that it will bring wholeness and wellness to your relationship. I wrote this book because I am convinced that it will be a useful instrument as another help in nurturing growth and development in a life worth living before God.

The Names: God, Christ and Lord will be used interchangeably throughout.

BEFORE YOU MAKE YOUR CHOICE

This book was born out of real counseling experiences with persons who were contemplating entering into a courtship relationship or had already been married for number of years.

The statements quoted were either made to me personally during an interview, a counseling session or were spoken by a partner to the other during our meetings. I have discovered that almost all of my clients were genuine with themselves, their partners and their relationship with the other. I have been able to deduce that they had well rounded lives, were well brought up and experienced love at home. I did not sense that they were trying to get away from home to enter into a relationship for which much thought was not given.

When you get into your marriage, it is vital that you create a home that will be a haven of love and security for you and your children. This means that you will give the Holy Spirit His place to enable you to keep your pledge "to love, honour and cherish each other." This atmosphere will enable your child or children to prepare for their inevitable departure into their own home.

CONTENTS

INTRODUCTION

As marriage partners, you will have to adapt to new roles; you will begin to think and act differently. You have both left your journey for a collective journey. Hitherto, you knew the individual plans you had. At the point of agreement, you both have set couple-select purpose plans.

Each spouse must consider new goals, which will inevitably bring moments of anxiety along with other wonders. These goals are set to remind you that you are not free-floating. There are known and unknown plans for your life. Yes! God's plans for your individual lives are still intact. He said to Jeremiah, *"I alone know the plans I have for you, plans to bring you prosperity and not a disaster and plans to bring about the future you hope for"* (Jeremiah 29:11 GNB).

As you set priorities and suggest various uses for your money, energy, health, and time, you will want God in the arena. In setting priorities for the marriage, remember that God wants your commitment, for He is committed to you and your covenant. This took place when you made your vows and promised to commit yourselves to the relationship with each other and with Him.

When you take the "two shall become one step," a tripartite relationship will be created comprising the husband, the wife, and God. God must be involved in the life of the marriage. Our Prayer Book makes the point that you receive God's grace, blessing, and guidance in your effort to discover your desired goals (What is Christian Marriage? The Book of Common Prayer, The Church in the Province of the West Indies 2007, p412).

Maintain from the very beginning these attributes:

Communication
Understanding

Honesty
Integrity
Trust

These attributes give impetus to the love life of the marriage.
Leaving your family homes to form your own home, you will experience
three things from individual homes.

i) qualities,
ii) values, and
iii) principles.

Some of these values will have commonality, while others will differ.
Whatever the case may be, adjustment on both sides will become
necessary.

BUILDING A STRONG FOUNDATION

Make Time For God

To experience God's love and faithfulness in the marriage, you must always spend time with God as individuals and as a couple. A marriage that God keeps stands on solid rock. It will pass through the waters and rivers and go down in the valley and climb the mountains. It will experience fire and many other damaging roads, but none of these will be victorious because the marriage is precious in the sight of God, Who is with the relationship all the way. Your time with God benefits the marriage. Be sure to set God as the priority for your marriage.

Like Joshua, you must declare, "...as for my family and me; we will serve the Lord" (Joshua 24:15 GNB). This declaration must be made for the marriage to meet its challenges and keep the vow which gives the opportunity and atmosphere for the wedding to give God His rightful place in the union.

"A marriage that is kept by God stands on a solid rock."

One forceful declaration was made by Anne Graham Lutz, who stated thus: "Years ago, I decided to follow Abraham's example and pursue God in a life of obedient faith one step at a time. Knowing God better each day has become The Magnificent Obsession of my life. My relationship with God is developed as I read His word, apply it to my life, then live it out on the anvil of my everyday experience!" (Anne Graham Lutz, The Magnificent Embracing the God-filled Life Journal, Zondervan 2009).

Spouses must be Positive at all Times

Spouses must be Positive at all Times
"Honour the wife as first in importance and the wife must respect the husband as first among equals for the marriage to work" (Emerson

Eggerichs p. 54). Every day one should cherish positive thoughts and perform positive actions. Never say to God, 'I cannot do this' or 'God, this is too hard.' Each day God's supplies await you for a safe journey. In that supply, every attribute you require for the day's tasks, decisions, and actions are within. God has never included discouragement in His daily gift for any of His children.

Make yourself available to God, and He will keep you intact as he makes sure that you are equipped for His journey. He gives words, actions, thoughts, and abilities necessary for the assigned tasks. In this way, individual skills will be maximized and used to advance His intended purpose.

You are made different than the other; and so, "The first task in a marriage for a couple is accepting, understanding and dealing with the basic difference that is with respect and love" (Thomas and Thomas, The Love a Wife Desires, The Respect a Husband Need, Integrity Publisher 2004, p. 173).

Problematic Times Are Times Of Learning

Isaac and Rebekah had what they thought was a severe problem. Rebekah did not show any sign of pregnancy for thirty-plus years. All kinds of questions went through the minds of Isaac and Rebekah. God told Abraham that his descendants would be numberless. So, how was this possible when Isaac remained childless? They asked, where have we wronged God? Why do we stay childless? Who will redeem all that we have? Who will take care of us in our old age? Shall we adopt a slave to be our heir?

Meanwhile, Isaac and Rebekah constantly prayed that they would be fruitful by having a child. David advises all to "wait on the Lord; be strong and take heart and wait for the Lord" (Psalm 27:14 NIV). This act of waiting makes Isaac and Rebekah attractive examples.

The problem of not having a child up to age thirty-nine was a learning experience for the couple. The lesson learned was "wait on the Lord, trust Him to act in His own time." Sure enough, God showed up in the thirty-ninth year of the marriage. Rebekah became pregnant, and after forty years, Isaac, who was 60 years became a father of two boys.

When you feel you cannot take much more and you think you are at the end of your rope or feel like life is closing in on you and God is nowhere to be found, remember, God never turns His back on any of His children. Be unbreakable! The apostle Paul was comforted when he said, "We are hard-pressed on every side, but not crushed, perplexed, but not in despair" (2 Cor. 4:8 NIV). And David assures that those who know the Lord will trust in Him, for He has never forsaken those who seek Him (Psalm 9:10 NIV).

In a discussion concerning a tree that bore not fruit, one man said to the other, "*Sir, leave it alone for one more year, and I will dig around it and fertilize it. If it bears fruit next year, fine. If not, then cut it down*" *(Luke 13:6)*. Are we troubled that our tree would not bear fruit? The tree reflects us when we examine our faithfulness in light of reality. We look at ourselves (the tree), and we expect to keep our marriage together, raise perfect children, make loyal friends, and perform our work without error (the fruit). When we fail and then become depressed, fearful, or anxious (rotten fruit), we want to cut ourselves. Like the tree owners, we want growth, but we judge ourselves quickly and harshly without taking the time to figure out the problem. We operate with truth and no grace. *(Changes That Heal, How To Understand Your Past To Ensure A Healthier Future, Dr. Henry Claud, p. 29 Zondervan 1992).*

A Peaceful Journey

A peaceful journey is experienced when the husband and wife walk with each other daily. When Christ walks with you, beautiful things happen because of His serenity. He is at peace amid chaos.

Christ's peace can only help when your whole house is open to Him. If your anteroom, living room, dining room, and kitchen are available to Him but not the bedroom and your inner chamber, you will never experience a peaceful journey. Remember, Christ knows what's in the house. He knows the private thoughts, fantasies, plans, and behaviors even when you fail to disclose them. Do not think you can hide that He has not seen your treasures representing the evidence of your authentic selves and beliefs.

In your relationship, look not for your interest but to the welfare of God; so that in the end, you will take back to Him only that which you genuinely gave away in His Name. The house that is not open to Christ is always in havoc with raging storms and longing for refuge, but the home that stands open realizes the peace and calmness which is always available. Open your house. Be still, and focus on God and His word. His peace will watch over you. Try to keep your home open; you will be glad you did.

The Use of Prayer in Marriage

Daily, ask God to use you as His servants, to minister and preserve each of you to be witnesses to His love. Never stop praying; pray together. Pray for your marriage to grow intimately daily. It is on your knees talking to God that your marriage will grow deeper and deeper. Pray for strength to overcome temptations. It is on your knees that you will hear God's instructions to enhance your marriage relationship.

… an interesting statistic shared by David McLaughlin in his wonderful series entitled *Role of the Man in the Family* that the divorce rate in America is at a minimum one out of two marriages. But the reported divorce rate among couples that pray together is about one in ten thousand. A pretty impressive statistic, even if you reduce it a thousandfold. It's a fact. He was praying together works. It is an (almost) guaranteed way to divorce-proof your marriage. So do it—every day. (Dr. Phil writes in his bestselling book, *Relationship Rescue*:)

> *"The house that stands open to God realizes the peace and calmness which is always available."*

God has the elements for a good marriage. They are numberless, and they help the marriage relationship to glow, grow and heighten. Indeed, a marriage with a constant prayer life receives God's guidance for the husband and wife. Prayer life increases wisdom and discernment for spiritual growth and blessings.

The process begins with a desire in the heart, a little thought in mind, a small light in the eye, and a small turning of spirit as you observe the example of someone else who pursued God - Moses maybe.

The Place of Worship in Marriage

"God created us in His image for the express purpose of giving Him the worship he deserves" (Jackie McCullough, Satisfaction of the Soul" Destiny Image Publishers, Inc. p. 56).

As the husband and wife blend their lives into one and the marriage grows stronger and stronger, the couple is reminded not to forget to work with God personally and collectively.

Bible study, prayer meeting, and worship must be given their rightful place in the marriage. The most beautiful thing a couple can do is to keep their marriage in the vigorous walk with Christ.

Spend time in worship; spend time with each other in prayer and praise, and spend personal quality time with God. These assure growth, development, wisdom, and knowledge for healthy living.

All that is necessary to complete a task comes from above. Believers of Christ cannot afford to settle for a mediocre approach to achieving a mission; such an attitude is not an option. Believers who walk daily with the Holy Spirit make it a priority to do chores from the heart – to the best of their ability. Christians cling to excellence as a priority in their lives. They cannot afford to settle for less. A Christian marriage is an example to others. The Apostle Paul advised, "Whatever you do, work at it with all your might, as working for the Lord, not for men" (Col. 3:23 NIV).

"One thing I do, forgetting those things which are behind and reaching forward to those things which are ahead I pressed toward the goal for the prize of the upward call of God in Christ Jesus" (Phil 3:13-14 KJV).

These words of Paul are a petition for the fullness of God's blessing; so that you can fulfill the potential He has for your life (Lotz p.16).

All and All (Bring Your True Self To The Marriage)

People should not enter a marriage relationship with reservations about each other or doubt whether the marriage will work. They should agree to leave and cleave. Leave all that will impair their lives. Cleave only to that which will have meaning when life is faced with all measures of seriousness. The seriousness of cleaving brings growth and bears an abundance of faith.

The partners in the marriage will know if their cleaving is serious by examining their hearts every morning. By so doing, they will not fool themselves or try to mislead each other. Examination of self brings the true self to the fore each day of the marriage. The husband and the wife should care only about what is the priority of each other's hearts.

Cleaving reminds the partners in the relationship that they are looking forward and not backward. The marriage is to be given all, not "nothing." The thing about marriage is its obligation to keep looking forward. Learn from past experiences and mistakes but never live in 'reverse.' Look forward to what will help the relationship continue to grow and climb to higher levels for the success of the marriage.

Each person in the marriage gives time and energy to help them become better cleavers and more vital partners. Lamenting over past pitfalls discourages and stresses its victims. Place them before you as stepping stones to press ahead. The finishing line is never behind; face it! Do everything possible that is worthy of the prize that one covets when one reaches the finishing line.

Seed Planting in Marriage

Paul, the apostle, advised the Galatians that every individual reaps what he sows; One cannot sow sinful nature and expect to reap a righteous one. Whoever plants a sinful nature will reap destruction; on the other hand, the one who sows to please God will reap eternal life (*see Gal. 6:7-8 NIV*).

The adage is correct "you cannot plant apple and reap pumpkin." The seed such a person sows in the marriage dictates the excellent fruit of the wedding. No one should spend their energy in selfish and sinful ways; that will not please God and certainly will not satisfy each other. Do you want to please God and your partner? Take time to study the good works of your partner.

> *"Whoever plants a sinful nature will reap destruction; on the other hand the one who sows to please God will reap eternal life (Gal. 6:7-8 MSG)."*

All through the Bible, there are examples of seed sowing and reaping. A farmer who plants reaps the harvest. The husband and wife must produce a good seed if they hope to reap the harvest in their family, career, business, and personal relationships *(Joel Osteen, Your Best Life Now—7 Steps to Living at your full Potential, p. 250)*.

Do not live self-centered lives; reach out to others. *"The reason many people are not growing is that they are not sowing"* (Osteen p. 250).

You Only Have One Partner

In his relationship with God, the Psalmist said, "Who have I in heaven but you? Earth has nothing I desire besides you. My body and my heart would fail me, but God is the strength of my heart and my portion forever" (Ps. 73:25-26 MSG).

Each partner in the marriage should know that the world has nothing outside of Godly principles and values to offer. Riches and success, fame, and health will bring some happiness, but only those things done for Christ will stand the test of time.

Attacks will occur; Satan is in every square inch of the marriage, especially since God is at the center. Hence, a conscious choice will daily hold God at the forefront of the pulse of the marriage. Stay focused! Stay focused on God and each other.

The world is hectic, so both husband and wife must be careful that the marriage stays on course. Both have to chart their course. They have to hold each other dear by honoring the stewardship of time in this area. A reasonable amount of time for careers, quality time for the home, each other, and the family is paramount.

If you want God to use you, you have to be willing to follow Him in uncomfortable places and do things you can't do on a natural level (Cymbaca Carol, Trusting God to Do What Only He can do *p25, Zondervan, 2001*).

The Place of Hope in the Marriage

Hope keeps the torch burning bright; its part in the marriage keeps everything in life worth living. It is the handle to open the door to the prize.

Hope brings relief and freedom from stress, which keeps you propelling onwards until victory is gained. The secret to this kind of life is – put your hope in Christ. Hope keeps the life charged with energy to stay upward and onward spiritually, emotionally, and physically.

Just as your hope in God is renewed daily, put your hope in your spouse daily. Only those who put their hope in God and each other will be successful in marriage. Remember, He will never lead you astray.

"Our thoughts and expectations yield tremendous power and influence in our lives. We don't always get what we deserve in life, but we usually get no more than what we expect; we receive what we believe. Unfortunately, this

principle works as strong in the negative as it does in the positive" (Osteen p.72).

Make Each Other Your Support Base

Your other half should be your support base. Your fears, pains, problems, insecurities, and anxieties should all find support from your floor. Each should be inviting the other to assist freely.

In the arms of the other, comfort, strength, and encouragement should be found because there is love for each other. One of the pledges of commitment each should make the other is the promise to help others carry their cross. So please continue to help; it makes life less stressful.

As you guard, protect and help each other, the assurance that someone cares speaks volumes. You know that your husband or your wife is not tired of hearing about your problems and wishes to help.

Being attuned to the other's feelings keeps the state of readiness awakened to supply extra strength and protection to your helpmate. Like an angel, your partner is available to guard, and you will not strike your feet against a rock. This kind of protection makes one feel so secure that they know not that they are protected, but the assurance that one is never alone will suffice.

The Psalmist David, who found himself in a similar state, made the point when he said, *"Even when the way goes through Death Valley, I'm not afraid when you walk by my side. Your trusting shepherd's crook makes me feel secure"* (Ps. 23:4 MSG).

Keep Reassuring Each Other

The marriage experience reaches its spiritual high when you read God's word. Be reminded that "God caused all holy scriptures to be written for our learning...and that we are to hear them, read, mark, learn and inwardly digest them, that we may embrace and hold fast the blessed hope of eternal life...in our Saviour Jesus Christ" (Book of Common

Prayer of the Province of West Indies, Collect for Sunday, Proper 28, page 181).

The persons who open themselves to receive garbage can only put out the trash. The mind filled with negative, unkind, impure thoughts will display these in their attitude and treat others. But those who serve their minds with right, pure and admirable things will be more positive and hopeful about life.

"Create a home where there is love, peace, harmony and pleasure. Resolve differences in love."

People who keep company with God and cry continually for His help will be encouraged and assured by the knowledge that they have God's support. There is no way that the couple would be alone in their walk down the complex corridor. God answers with His guidance and the assurance of His love. Here is the courage to face whatever is ahead.

"As husband and wife, you can profoundly influence the life of each other by the words and things you do. As husband and wife, you can set the direction for your family. With words and actions, you have the ability to help fashion the future of anyone you have influenced" (Osteen p. 133).

Have a Strong Foundation

One who is looking for strength, help, and hope will not find it in substances such as drugs, tranquilizers, alcohol, food, or drink. There is no foundation in these. We thank God for friends, but we cannot use friends as our foundation. Friends can turn up to a point, but beyond that point, there is a void. Oh yes, some friends do encourage us on the right path. Remember that Jesus had friends, and one denied Him, one betrayed Him, while the others fled from him in time of need. Friends sometimes do not go all the way—Jesus went all the way to Calvary and conquered. He will always bring the vessel to port.

"No one is perfect, and no marriage is perfect. You will both continue to make mistakes and slip up in your attempt to make a great relationship. But you can go a long way towards safety, closeness, and intimacy when you root out the

problem underlying the repeated patterns in your marriage. When you resolve the issues, you should see great change and progress." Paul commended young Timothy for the strong foundation inculcated in him from birth. (Osteen p. 30). (2Tim. 1:1-5 NIV).

Good Marriages

All marriages are good, but some unions are better than others. Create a home where there is love, peace, harmony, and pleasure. Resolve differences in attachment. Agree, disagree, agree to disagree, but avoid disagreeableness. Disagreeableness is the seed sown to produce divorce.

The couple that shows respect for each other and resolves their differences of opinion will always model a proper way to treat each other and work in harmony to fulfill dreams and aspirations.

Good marriages are made by the couple who shows strength to help each other, stand together to tackle what may come and seek to help each other in the best way possible. This life stands out supreme before all eyes.

There is no ideal person with whom the husband and wife should be compared. Neither of you can or will be someone else. When you are yourself, you are a prince or a princess in your own right. It only takes the kiss of your love to awaken them. *"If you stop showing compassion and love for the one you are with, then your dream of a good marriage can not come true. You can live happy, though imperfectly ever after." (Rescue Your Love Life: Change Those Dumb Attitudes and Behaviours That Will Sink Your Marriage, Dr. Henry Cloud & Dr. John Townsend 2005, Thomas Nelson, p.72).*

The Place of In-laws in Marriage

Scripture sets the conditions under which a marriage should exist. It declares, *"Therefore a man [a woman as well] leaves his [her] father and mother and embraces his wife [her husband]. They become one flesh" (Genesis*

2:24 The Message Bible). The husband and wife leave all relatives at home and form a home solely with each other.

The man or woman should meet each other's parents and siblings when possible. This meeting is not for approval for Tom to marry Jane or for Sue to marry Harry. It is for the entire family to get to know the person who will become a permanent part of it. Additionally, the man or woman should have a firsthand experience of his wife or husband's family. The significance of getting to know the family on both sides is because "your in-laws are not just anyone. Those who are connected to their spouse through physiological dynamics" *(Pastor Faith Oyedepo "Faith in Defense of Freedom" Introduction).*

From the onset, husband and wife should agree with each other on all relationships with other family members. This agreement may include time, assistance, and attention to be shared. *(Theodore K. Pitt, "Premarital Counseling Handbook for Ministers," Judson Press Valley Forge p. 174).* Families should enjoy rapport that is second to none. Simultaneously, maintaining their distance and keeping a "bird's eye" view on the relationships while doing all in their power to make sure that "coherent boundaries" of love, respect, kindness, honor, and distance. Observing the boundaries set should not be based on control, taking sides, manipulating, and influencing selfish gain.

The Place of Children in Marriage

Not all married couples want children to be part of their family, and that decision has to be respected by others. However, there is a place in the marriage for children biological or adoption for those who desire. The husband and wife should agree with each other's mutual responsibilities, and the time they would independently spend with those children while raising them *(Theodore K. Pitt, "Premarital Counseling Handbook for Ministers" Judson Press Valley Forge p.174).* This family context gives the children a place of security, stability, and love. Children in marriage bring to bear on the couple the value of fidelity between them and children. We ought to remember that with all the *"pressure on family life today, it seems all the more important to underscore the value of permanence in the marital relationship to children" (Thomas and Thomas, "Beginning Your Marriage" ACTA Publications 1994, p. 60).*

ENCOURAGEMENT

Be Wise in Spending Your Time

Ours is a two income world; and it is taken for granted that both husband and wife will need to have jobs. Although both parents being away from home can result in problems that the couple did not bargain for. The trials of everyday life can be so overwhelming that the couple may not be able to spend quality time together *(Thomas and Thomas p.150)*.

What do you spend your time doing? Where do you spend your time? Do your friends get the greater part of your time over coffee, the Internet or the telephone?

Do you both work? When you get home, does one lounge while the other is busy doing household chores such as cooking, washing and the like?

Managing the home is the responsibility of both of you in this instance. The responsibility of the husband and wife should be shared. This certainly gives each other equal opportunity to be with the other, doing things that are profitable and too, it reserves energy for the other at your prime time.

Do this together. No arguments, especially over trivialities. Be responsible, as adults not as kids fighting over tops and watching to see the amount of work the other is doing. The work of the household should be on the shoulders of both.

A sweet spirit accomplishes a lot more for your relationship and the marriage life. Answer each other's questions or comments without complaining or arguing. Would that help the situation? Be gentle. That is a better idea.

Be Content on the Journey

A Marriage life should be compared to that of a baby re-boxing in the mother's arms. He has had his bath, a bottle of food, diaper changed, and is lying quite comfortably in Mom's warmth. God has done all that for the marriage, and the couple - husband and wife are in the Lord's arms, which offer complete comfort.

Reflected in the minds and faces are peace and contentment. There is nothing that is found missing in the marriage. If enjoyment is present, the marriage is in a smooth sailing mood.

The marriage that walks in godliness and contentment is aware that each new day is a gift from God. Whatever you have in your life comes from God. Therefore let God take complete control and let go of His protection, guidance, love, peace, and contentment. God led you to the marriage, so put your trust in Him to guide you through it.

"Remember thee! Yea from the table of my memory. I'll wipe away all trivial records and thy commandments all alone shall live Within the book and volume of my brain unmixed with laser-matter" (Hamlet By William Shakespeare, Act I, Scene V, p. 4).

Spur Each Other On

Pray together. Work things out together. Laugh together. Play together. Be creative. Respect each other's space. Hold one another's interest at heart. The joy of living together as husband and wife encourage one another to try new things and explore their talents and gifts.

Encourage each other! When the wife cooks your favorite meal, let her know how pleasant and how she makes you feel. If the husband bakes his usual pie, make him feel elated by having a second helping. Oh, how you enjoyed every bit of it!

Use every opportunity to strengthen how you feel about each other. Your expression of appreciation opens up avenues for better companionship and reinforces love and security.

Work together on a project. As you head to head and solve one problem after another, you become heart to heart *(Dr. Emerson Eggerichs, Love & Respect, Thomas Nelson 2004 p. 295).* Prepare and work tenderly together. Wash up together after dinner. Enjoy the pleasure of serving each other than at meal time. Working together is terrific, especially when you have similar ideas and values.

It is a pleasure when you work through a difference of opinion. The food tastes sweeter, and life becomes less complicated.

Working together calls for sharing – share your time, heart, ear, hand, preferences, and desires, especially when it brings joy to the other.

Married couples have a support system: if one stumbles, the other is there to help lift and hold up the fallen. It means that one is covered positively. It takes the power of two to make love stronger and live out their purpose in the world. Hence the writer wrote, *"It is better to have a partner than go it alone. Share the work, share the wealth, and if one falls, the other helps, but if there is no one to help, tough!" (Ecc. 4: 9,10 MSG)*

You chose each other to share your pain, grief, friends, kindness, compassion, gentleness, patience, joy, happiness, and the like. As you share these qualities, warm heart the other extends to make life hospitable and comfortable.

One's true qualities encompass all the values and much more for a wholesome personality that can only breathe an aroma to permeate the heavenly atmosphere.

What are Some of the Things Consistency Requires?

Hold each other in your heart. It shows that the presence of love and respect is in the marriage's heart. Be consistent with each other's feelings. Consistency simply means that one will be one's self no matter the circumstance. Be disciplined at all times. Find out what is wrong and fix it. *"Daily watch the little conflicts that can ruin the vineyard" (Song of Songs 2:15 MSG).*

Many people become disillusioned when persons around them seem to have no standard in behavior and conduct. Consistency is not one-sided; both parties must not only know of the Word but should practice it in their personal lives. Consistency is a Sunday to Sunday affair; it is the living out of one's Christian life in the sight of all.

"No one can build a chasm between you and God's love."

For consistency, everyone must make God's Word a noticeable presence in their lives to live and speak all week long. Such practice proclaims the Word of God every day to all and sundry.

Pass on your Heritage

"it only takes a spark to get us all going...Pass It On" (Song by Texan Baptist 1969).

Marriage demands a permanent desire to share everything. In a marriage, both parties bring from their home their idiosyncrasies: likes, dislikes, styles, worship, attitudes, mannerisms, favorites, feelings, and preferences. In this new setting, each will influence the other, thus making that marriage unique.

There is an opportunity to pass on the lineage of the faith ingrained in the family environment—the opportunity to pass on the truths and joys of Christian standards responsibly.

When your partner sees positiveness at work, they will be much more likely to emulate that way of life for themselves. Of primary importance among those is the application of the gospel incorporated in your life. Such a lifestyle awaits the opportunity to be passed on to the next home that your children will build.

Stay on Course

Do not let work, bills, too much money or the lack of it, relationship problems, busyness, and stress get you off course. Paul has some advice, *"With God on our side, how can we lose?" (Romans 8:31).* God has put everything on the line for us. He embraced our condition and exposed Himself to the worst, and sent His own Son. What else would He not deliberately and gladly do for us? Who can be so brave as to mess with what God has put in place and His chosen will? No one will so dare to point one finger against the one who died and rose to life for us. Hence no one can build a chasm between you and God's love. No trouble, no hardship, no hatred, no hunger, no homelessness, no bullying, no threat, no backbiting, nothing beyond one's imagination can separate you from God.

God never gives you a set of blueprints for your life all at one time. It is doubtful that God ever did this. God may not even explain the essential next step. While on the path of marriage, you have to trust God and confidently follow His instructions. Even when you do not understand life as it unfolds *(Copeland, Gloria: God's Majestic Plan for your Life. Keys to Fulfilling your Destiny, Berkley Publication Group, p.167-168).*

Do Not Run Away From Life

The prophet Elijah ran away from life. He crawled into a cave and begged God to take away His life *(see 1 Kings 19:10 GNB).* At times things may get so rough that you want to pull your head, hands, and feet into a hole and just be tucked away for life.

Be reminded that there is no way to hide from God's presence. The Psalmist has so instructed, *"Is there any way I can go toward your spirit? To be out of your sight? If I climb to the sky, you are there! If I go underground, you are there! If I flew on morning's wings to the far western horizon, you would find me in a minute. You are already there waiting! Then I said to myself, Oh, He even sees in the dark! ..." (Psalm 139:7-11 MSG.)*

There is only one safe place for your marriage - under God's wings. There the Psalmist says God will hide you with His feathers, and under His wings, you will find refuge; His faithfulness will be your shield and stay *(Psalm 91:4 GNB)*.

Once you choose to hold to God, you will find refuge and peace; if you decide to stay unprotected on the ground, you will be tossed about by the waves of this world and bear the consequences of that status.

Withstand the Test of Time

Cherish the value of what will last—God's Word in you. Negative things will all come to an end, but the Word of God will assist you to stand the test of time, for it is the only thing that continues forever.

God's presence is constant. His promises hold up against all odds. His strength is always present. You will never move beyond God's reach. You are always in God's space. So the Hymn writer is correct when he penned the lyrics:

"Your Partnership should take first place as you walk with each other."

> *Under His wings, Oh what precious enjoyment!*
> *There will I hide till life's trials are o'er;*
> *Sheltered, protected, no evil can harm me;*
> *Resting in Jesus, I'm safe evermore*
> *(Cushing, Under His Wings, 541).*

The Psalmist cemented it when he referred to God's substantial outstretched arms protecting you because under them, you are perfectly safe, and they fend off all harm *(see Psalm 91:4 GNB)*.

Openness in Marriage

Do your best to be open and honest during discussions. Your transparency will encourage your partner to do the same. *(Dion, Jennifer: Fire Proof your Marriage, Participant's Guide, 2nd Edition 2008, Outreach Publication p. 7).* Communication is vital in this relationship. The more often you communicate, the more relaxed you become to relate to each other; and the essential matters will be resolved.

TEAMWORK

Give up Selfishness: No More "I" but "We"

Appreciate each other and share what you admire most about the other. Roll out the red carpet for each other. All Christians who give up past lives have been taught to give up individualism to disciple Christ. Luke advised that *"Anyone who does not give up everything he has, cannot be Christ's disciple" (Luke 14:33 NIV)*.

Wisdom dictates that the *"heart of the wise instructs his mouth, and adds persuasiveness to his lips" (Proverbs 16:23 NIV)*. From the onset, the husband and wife have to set goals and priorities. This is the first step in forgetting self and working for the good of both. This attitude makes priority setting relatively easy.

Belonging to each other must be first; way ahead of other responsibilities, desires, or even priorities. Once the importance of giving up everything, each for the other, is established, all other goals will fall in place.

Your partnership should take first place as your walk with each other. Whatever does not enhance the one goal of assisting each other to fulfill your dreams and aspirations is simply not worth doing.

It is essential for the husband to know his wife and for the wife to know her husband. This relationship shows each other Who Christ is. Life of this nature does not happen by accident. Each day in the marriage is an opportunity to choose a life pattern that will enhance your relationship. God gives each the ability to decide to live one for the other.

As the choice is made constantly, the decision is affirmed for the longevity of the marriage. Husband and wife live for each other to put the Jesus of the union into perspective.

Paul, the apostle, was pleased with his choice and was determined to make the marriage with Christ a life work. Paul pledged to keep the celebration going because he knew how it would all turn out. For him, whatever God wants to accomplish will be done. This will come to pass through faithful prayers and the generous response of the Spirit of Jesus Christ. By this, he was eager to go the entire course of the marriage. Any unfortunate situation that happened to him made his walk with Christ more accurate, so he declared, "For me to live is Christ and *die is gain" (Phil. 1:21 NIV).*

In the marriage, nothing is more important to the wife than the husband and vice versa. Nothing is more important than showing how important they are by living to satisfy the other. This does not happen overnight or by accident. Every day, each will determine how to relate to the other or the action or reaction. In other words, every day, the choice that is made to live for each other is for the better.

"...partners in the marriage make daily the decision through positive living, to make the marriage work until death parts.

Just as Paul made his choice for eternity, so too should the partners in the marriage make daily the decision through positive living, to make the marriage work until death parts. Every Christian couple should resolve to make their lives in union with Christ meaningful, making it essential to live in collaboration within the marriage bond. That puts a Christian marriage into perspective.

Bring Your Gifts to the Marriage

No matter how hard it gets, husbands love your wives, and wives, love your husbands.' Your love life should always be on the highway; it should never branch off into individual lanes. Besides bringing yourselves to each other in the marriage bond for Christ to join you, get love. Come to the relationship with God. Pray to Him, study His Word, and give Him yourselves; He will prepare you to give yourselves to each other sincerely, earnestly, and wholeheartedly, and your gift of money for the advancement of His Work will be natural.

Practice demonstrates that what is mine is God's and my husband's, and what is my wife's and mine are God's and mine. Find the meaning of God's command in Genesis, *"A man leaves his father and mother and joins to his wife they both belong to each other"* (Gen. 2:24 GNB).

One leaves behind his possessive ties with his biological family and joins the other to be in oneness to care and share their all. The Anglican Marriage Service vow states, *"All that I am I give to you and all that I have I share with you within the love of God, Father, Son, and Holy Spirit"* (The Book of Common Prayer p. 235).

The giving of husband and wife in marriage is to understand that all that they are, and all that they have, are gifts from God and that their giving of themselves to Him and each other helps to spread God's word throughout the world. That way of giving is God's commanded priority for the marriage bond.

"Sit back and listen and learn from each other for the way forward."

Will Times Get Tough?

The apostle Paul advised that husband and wife must stay in love no matter how hard it gets *(see Col. 3:19)*. Life in Christ has never been a pie in the sky by and by; or an enjoyable sweet lullaby rest from now until eternity. There will be hills, ravines, and plains to walk. Life, on the whole, is challenging. There will be the tough decisions and the hard questions. The answer will always come from the dictates of a Godly conscience.

The marriage life has not been nor will it ever be spared from the life mentioned above. There will be stresses stemming from unemployment, marriage road blocks, the children following their opinions, health, friendships, in-laws, and so forth.

Keep On Track

Show each other unconditional love and respect. In marriage, there should not be 'tit for tat.' Do not point out every mistake your other half makes. Be patient with each other. Your patience shows how smart you are; it shows your wisdom. Do not keep a score of who did what and to whom, and how often. Keeping score of every wrong drive the other away; your company is not appreciated any longer.

Do unto the other as you would want them to do unto you. We are reminded that *"a man's wisdom gives him patience; it is to his glory to overlook an offense" (Prov. 19:11 NIV).*

Consistency in Marriage

You ought to know what will exasperate your other half! Make every effort to do what is right within a Godly conscience. These principles and values should be the tools that govern the rubrics of marriage life. Do not confuse the other person into doing inconsistent things. This behavior only serves to disrupt the smooth sailing of the marriage ship.

Consistency in marriage calls for the husband and wife reminding each other whose they are, Christ's children; and as such, their actions must be in response to His relationship with them

Carry Each Other's Burdens

To carry each other's burdens, you have to be in love with each other. Remember, *"love is not a feeling, it is a choice, a commitment" (Eggerichs p. 98).* Whatever hurts one should hurt the other. Whatever appeals to one's heart should gladden the other. Study each other so that you can detect when they are hurting or rejoicing. It would be best if you kept goodwill in your hearts.

When Jesus' disciples were under stress, He intervened and inquired of others what was wrong. He said to Peter, *"Satan wants to sift you like wheat, stay focused, I have prayed for you and when you find the strength to share it with the others" (Luke 22:31 MSG).*

God placed you in a relationship with your differences to keep the marriage alive, warm and encouraging. Whatever good there is to share, satisfy your hunger and do the job.

Be Ready to Learn From Your Partner

Endeavor not to be harsh or full of evil in your dealings with each other *(see 1 Samuel 25:3 MSG)*. You do not come into the marriage complete with knowledge in every subject matter. You have to take marriage life step by step, day by day. You do not come to the marriage knowing all about marriage. You can attend classes from time immemorial; you still have to learn what marriage is from personal experience.

A person can be taught how to fly an aircraft from age two until age ninety-nine, but unless they get into the helicopter and fulfill the required number of hours, they are never considered pilots.

Marriage foundation can never be learned and realized until the man and woman take the reins and share their lives in that bond. So be ready to be teachable. The Psalmist begged God to *"Teach me your ways O Lord; make them known to me. Teach me to live according to your truth, for you are my God, who saved me. I always trust in* **"Communicate all** *you." (Psalm 25:4-5 NIV.)* Sit back and listen **the time.."** and learn from each other for the way forward.

Stand Firm With God And Each Other

It is the god who will touch and keep the hearts of a married couple. The marriage that is in God's hands will daily be reconciled. No matter the problem which stands in your face, stand firm. Moses advised his people to stand with God. *"Do not be afraid, stand firm, and you will see the deliverance the Lord will bring you today" (Ex. 14:13 GNB).*

At times, life is such that there is a natural reaction to frantically try to ward off the problem or solve it yourself. Moses did not tell his people to do that in their crisis; He encouraged them to stand firm. The people obeyed, and marvelous things happened when Israel saw God do a miracle. You need to take Moses' advice; stop the scurrying around; do not back away; stand firm and see what God will do for you.

You Are Never Alone

Keep your divine appointments daily. This is the key to daily growth and effectiveness in sharing life-long happiness. Paul reminds us that *"God has poured out His love into our hearts by the Holy Spirit, whom He has given us"* (*Romans 5:5 MSG*). The Holy Spirit gives *"stackability."* Whatever comes your way, good resides in it.

Pause and give God thanks that you are making it through difficulties. Each morning you rise, take your steps of life, for you are on the Master's mission. Yes! God is beside you all the way. Nothing is more significant than your God. We would never understand His greatness because He is more important than whatever we have to face. He helps at all times and will give you His care.

Indeed, we can never know one another as wholly as our Lord knows us. Yet, because marriage is to be the imitation of Christ's love for His Church, we are to understand our mates with a knowledge approaching Christ's. We are to be alive to say, *"I know my own, and my own know me"* (*Achtenmeier, E (1976), The Committed Marriage, p. 134, Westminster Press*). *"Thou knowest me right well"* (*Psalm 134:14*).

Your Spouse Comes First

You thought a lot about each other before or else you will not be married now. Keep it that way. This is the cherishing part of your marriage; keep warming each other with acceptance and affection. *(Getting Married, Family Doctor Publication. Published by British Medical Association. 1977 p.7).*

In most cases, husbands who are in love with their wives; and wives who are in love with their husbands will move toward each other when they feel unloved. Make the other top on your priority list. Do not live inconsiderately and insensitively. These are unloving behaviors and make the other feel less human. So avoid the lecture when you walk in through the door. "We need to talk; we need to talk right now! Let us sit down and talk." Communicate all the time to avoid this stage.

Do not be a doormat for your husband or your wife. Do not fail to use your intelligence and leadership abilities to direct the conversation into a meaningful one; so that the result **would be beneficial** to both. Neither of you is superior or inferior, and do not ignore your hurts and vulnerabilities.

Maintain a respectful attitude during a conflict; it will never render you powerless.

It Is Not Always About Me

You are not single any longer; you are half of the pair. You have promised to love, comfort, honor, and cherish each other; through good and bad times. *(Getting Married, Family Doctor Publication. Published by British Medical Association, 1977 p. 7).*

The way you come across can be unloving. If you are conscious of that attitude being displayed, ask your spouse if you gave that impression so that you will not always be on the defensive; and try to avoid the expression, "It is always my fault, or it is always me, I am always to be blamed."

Happy People Are Givers

From the very beginning, you have committed to giving all that you are and all that you have within the love of God, Father, Son, and Holy Spirit. *(The Book of Common Prayer, CPWI, 1995 p. 335).*

While there may be some activities in life that are in question, giving to others is not one of them—showing acts of kindness and being altruistic are not activities we have to be corned. If you want to increase your happiness, spend some of your heart, mind, and soul - even your money - on others. *(Dr. Henry Cloud, The Law of Happiness pp. 20-21, Howards Books, 2011).*

UNDERSTANDING CHRIST'S ROLE

Core Trust

Trusting your partner is foundational. The husband and the wife must trust each other. They should know where their confidence lies. Cleaving in the marriage has at its core the element of trust. Trust is the underlay that gives strength to the challenges of the marriage bond. Indeed, we can never know one another as wholly as our Lord knows us. Yet, because marriage is to be the imitation of Christ's love for His church, we are to understand our mate with a knowledge approaching His. We ought to be able to say, 'I know my own, and my own know me.' Thou knowest me right well. *(The Committed Marriage, Elizabeth Achtenmeier, p. 134, Westminister Press 1976).*

The opinion of another should only be counted if it was agreed that both would seek it and should only be relied upon to assist the parties in reaching a workable conclusion of which they are solely the author.

Trust should never be put in material things. Success and importance do not come from possessions. As is mentioned above, career, drug substances, and the apparent success of others all have their places, but trust in them calls for danger. The only sure foundation is satisfied with what one has and who one is. Trust reveals where one's confidence lies. They should be worthy of the other's confidence. The marriage is blessed when there is trust in God and trust between the husband and the wife. Be happy with your partner and find joy in the choice you made. Pretty and graceful as a deer, let her charms keep you satisfied. Let her cover you with her love *(see Proverbs 5:18,19 GNB).*

Love Despite

There will be times when you fail; here is some advice, *"A righteous man falls seven times, and he rises again" (Proverbs 24:16MSG).* The marriage is like a baked cake that gets broken. Gently the broken pieces are placed back together, sometimes layer upon layer or component by work; then icing is pasted around and upon it. There the problem is covered up and well smoothed in. After this exercise, the heart of the cake maker is gladdened; others who do not know what went on with the cake's life see only the wonderful decorated cake. You see! The evidence of the problem lies underneath.

> *"The best of all the elements in the marriage bond is prayer."*

Love does just what the icing of a cake does. The marriage relationship has its mistakes, selfishness, unkindness, and other thoughtless things that just mess up from time to time. It does no good covering over the relationship with money, pride, or arrogance. The safe and best way to cover the problem is with love. Love will not intentionally damage a relationship or hurt someone, but when it is broken accidentally and love is present, the healing process occurs.

God Does Not Change

"In the ocean *of conflict, the marriage will never sink."* The boat may be destroyed, but the marriage will be saved *(see Acts 27:22 GNB)*. There are changes in the world. Changes in hair styles, dress, mood, atmosphere, temperature, but there is one who never changes. It is said that life "is variable in every aspect," but there is one whose heart is fixed, and He is Christ. As God takes up residence in the marriage, He brings the stability necessary to anchor the ship. He is the basis for the hope of marriage.

Marriage relationships are not on the turf of shifting sand. Christ blessed it. He helps them to keep their character, power, wisdom, justice, and truth. He is its refuge and strength. Yes, He is the stronghold in times of trouble, and this will never change. The God of the marriage never changes *(see Malachi 3:6 GNB)*.

Model Marriages

The model marriage stays united *"so that they are no longer two but one. Man must not separate, what God has joined together" (Matthew 19:6 GNB)*. A marriage like this, if emulated, is the kind that gets respect.

Married couples who make wise decisions and live their lives to show good judgment and discernment encourage others to live their lives similarly. A model marriage ought to be exemplary to marriages that are in their infancy.

What Place Should Prayer Take In Marriage

Scripture declares: *If any is in trouble, he should pray. If one is happy, he should sing songs of praise (James 5:13 GNB)*. Some couples enter into marriage wondering if the marriage life will work. This is fear at its core. Matthew reminds all not to fear but believe *(see Matt 5:36 GNB)*. The alternative to fear is trusting God, taking Him at His word, and believing that He stands with you.

Whatever God leads you to, He will guide you through. One's first response to problems is to turn to God, to cry out to God in prayer. He will give guidance, comfort, and relief. Remember that a relationship with God makes the impossible possible and works in the uphill climb and the downhill slide.

There is consolation in the hands of the Psalmist, *"I have been young and now am old, I have never seen the dependent on God-forsaken, or his ancestors are begging in the street" (Ps 37:25 GNB)*.

Keep your shortcomings before the throne of grace. He will work with you on your knees to overcome them. Nothing is sweeter than when the husband and wife fall on their knees *"with their face to the rising sun"* (Hymn, "Let us break bread" African American Spiritual.), lifting each other to the throne of God.

Prayer keeps the marriage constant before God, who surrounds, protects, guides, and keeps intact the activities and the stance on the choices made. So prayer gives the wisdom to face each other and the way forward.

Never be too busy to stay close to God. No matter how busy you are, do not let your devotional time and your prayer time with God slide (*come apart with God*. ABHP)

If you have much time on hand or no time on hand, you need quality time with your Maker. This is the time for God's guidance both at work and at leisure.

Marriage has many good elements to help it to grow as your love relationship develops. It is worth repeating, the best of all the ingredients in the marriage bond is prayer. Pray for each other. Ask God to guide each of you. He will give you a daily dose of wisdom and discernment. You will also be given spiritual growth and God's blessing for the way ahead.

"Do not speak about how to live the marriage life; live the life and someone will get the message."

Pray for profound, intimate experiences and your relationship in general to blossom with fragrant oneness. Pray for strength to withstand life trials and temptations. Pray for the clarity of scripture as you conduct your personal and family devotions.

Prayer will help you see very clearly where in life's journey God will lead you to be His servant, minister, and witness His love and grace. St. Paul so advises us never to stop praying *(see 1 Thess. 5:17 GNB)*.

Prayer must be central to the life of the husband and wife if they are serious *"about embracing [their] magnificent obsession" (Lotz p. 62)*.

Marriage Is Not An 'Eye For An Eye' Business

Do not take revenge on each other when wronged *"...but I tell you to love and pray for those who persecute you. You must be perfect just as your Father is perfect" (Matthew 5:38-48 GNB)*. When everything is excellent and going well with relationships, it would seem "like pie in the sky by and by." When the relationship hits a bump when one is hurt intentionally or not, what will be the response? Does one turn to an "eye for an eye" principle and seek to get even one with the other?

Whether applied secretly or otherwise, this philosophy will be tantamount to selfishly forcing justice. God's justice is much different, it calls for the injured to turn the other cheek, depend on Him, live in love, and He will be vindicated.

God's principle brings out the best life for both partners who walk His walk and talk His talk. The life He requires encourages both parties to make the other a better person.

Life becomes more meaningful when one has the confidence that they are in a relationship where each other cares, believes in, and is busy serving their interest. Such a state of mind encourages the recipient to respond in like manner to others.

It is the act of kindness that gives the impetus for good deeds one after the other. When you are spurred towards love and good deeds, the world gets to know the full power of love. Here is what God's love does, it grows in the heart - in the relationship, and it reaches others, thus making the world a better place.

"The instruction manual for marriage is the Bible."

The writer to the Hebrew people advised them to *"spur one another on towards love and good deeds" (Hebrews 10:24 NIV)*.

Marriage Life Is Not Only For The Couple

Marriage life is not for the couple only. It is also a life that should encourage others to enter that way of life. Marriage is not only for Christians. It is for all male/female couples.

Jesus' statement, *"From the beginning God made them male and female, therefore when a man leaves his father and mother and cleaves to his wife, they are no more two but one and should not be divided"* (see Mark 10:6-9 GNB). The writer of the first account of the gospel reminds all that marriage life brings a deep sense of commitment when couples enter the marriage arena (*see Matthew 19:3-12* GNB).

What Jesus implies is that the couple should go about their life, endeavoring to entice each other to keep their love life on the front burner so that others will be impressed with it. Jesus went about spending much time with the "undesirables" of His time so that they would not get comfortable in their zone where others all look the same, believe the same, and share the same social standards.

What is the catch? That all will remember that there is a whole world full of men and women who should follow the example set. Each couple should realize that God depends upon them to give the marriage bond its rightful place in His Kingdom.

Action speaks louder than words. Do not speak about living the married life; live the life, and someone will get the message. It is the reality of living the marriage life that demonstrates how others can find happiness in that state.

> *"If trust in God is lacking, then trust is lacking in the relationship."*

If husband and wife live face to face with God's love, professing their faith in God daily, their action will show those who are waiting to cause trouble for their relationship that God is piloting their marriage towards success.

You Have Made Your Choice

IF you walk into the marriage, you have resolved to live in the union. It does not mean that your daily life will be about achieving "big events;" it is about "a quiet peace," steady progress, a gentle person, a quiet heart, and steadfast love. *(Roy Lessin, His Footsteps, My Pathway, 2007, Christian Art Gift, RSA)*. It is God's choice to have called you. You being here is not a mistake; you are exceptional because you are God's child. God – the creator of all things animate and inanimate chose you. You are His, and nothing can be more special than that.

In the marriage, both of you made up your minds to share your lives. The agreement is yours. You made a choice to live until death parts you. You did not make that choice to sit quietly for the rest of your life or to live a selfish life.

"The answer to your strength is God."

The life you choose with each other is one that you can fully enjoy with the person who shares your space. It is a life that is not covered with darkness but full of light, love, joy, happiness, and cooperation to weather the rough times in unity.

Here is where each partner's skills are allowed for the uniqueness of gifts and talents to come to the fore for success. If such contributions are allowed to take their course in patience and diligence, then the marriage will glow. Each person should encourage the other to keep the zeal and enthusiasm that began in courtship. Such excitement and joy keep the marriage burning.

Be Vigilant

Encourage your partner to get busy from day one to keep the interest they began the marriage. The minute you lose interest in your purpose in the marriage, the sooner interest in each other dies. The eagle, which sees its prey from the top of the mountain, never loses sight of its location until it swoops down upon it. Keep watching the things that serve to build the marriage, and always grasp the positives that move upwards.

Do not Pour cold water or more matter. If the situation is allowed to fester without appropriately handling it, however daunting it may sound, the marriage will not experience Solomon's advice. He states, *"Eat and drink until you are drunk with love. Solomon continues,* But *my* vineyard is all mine, and I'm keeping it to myself. You can have your vast vineyards, Solomon, you and your greedy guests! *(Song of Songs 8:12 MSG).*

God's Instruction Manual

The instruction manual for marriage is the Bible. The Bible corrects, teaches, challenges, trains, and fills every individual to do the work God has ordained. The Bible calls upon those it instructs to share God's teaching with others. "Couples should not doubt the exalted nature of God's love and the high standard of moral excellence to which Christians are called in both the Old and New Testament scriptures." (Edmeade, James (1994) Before Your Divorce, p11, Companion Press).

No couple should enter into marriage ill-equipped. Peruse the tools, know the tools, apply the tools, and watch the marriage life overflow with success. The tools used skillfully and cleverly will hold when things go wrong and problems creep through the back door. Thus, discouragement will not find an abiding place.

In the tough times of life, God will never forget the marriage. So in using the tools, always remember that God is in the background cheering you on with His grace.

You Are Special To God

The Psalmist declares, *"...For I am fearfully and wonderfully made; miracles are thy works...that my soul knoweth right well"* (Psalm 139:14 GNB). Every day God is watching you with the apple of His eye! Just because you are unique in His eyes. *"For him that toucheth you, toucheth the apple of His eye" (Zechariah 2:8bKJV).*

The writer of Genesis tells us how extraordinary human beings are to God. *"God created man in His image, in the image of God created He male and female created He them" (Genesis 1:27GNB).* It is not a coincidence that the Psalmist says, we are the apple of God's eye; and would hide us under His wings just as a mother hen hides her chicks under her wings, (Psalm 17: 8 KJB)

We are to keep in daily contact with God by trusting in His love and protection from the evil one. Since you are created in the image of God, act like Him. Have standards like Him. Do not compromise your values. Live up to the high standards of your created order. *(Jackie McCullough, "Satisfaction of the Soul" Destiny Image Publishers, Inc. p. 162).*

The Marriage That Trusts God Is Safe

When a couple has peace, joy, ability and sees God in everything, they sleep well, are healthy, and enjoy life to its fullest. All these sweeten the relationship with God.

If trust in God is lacking, then faith is lacking in the relationship. Stress then takes the place of God, eats away at your being and your relationship with God and each other. Stress is a powerful tool that Satan uses to detour God's people to another highway.

There is a saying, "when in Rome do as the Romans do," that does not apply because different cultures permit many sexual partners. Sometimes untoward behaviors are not licensed for Christians to ignore the demands for right living specified by the Word of God. To hide behind certain customs and cultures only violate God's law for marriage *(Edmeade p. 3).*

God's Strength Not Yours

David spoke for all when he acknowledged God as his shepherd and provider for all his needs. God, he said, sent him down into lush meadows, and down there, he found God's pool from which to drink.

Zechariah reminded his readers that his success as a prophet was not according to his power and might, but such success depended upon the Spirit of God *(see Zechariah 4:6)*.

God is true to His word, for He allowed David to catch his breath and sent him on the right path. Yes, the course went through a dark valley, but he was not afraid, for God walked by his side and his shepherd staff made him feel secure. Divine grace was provided to him in the face of his enemies. He was well fortified because enough was on his plate, and his cup of drink ran over into the basin.

God's care and love chased after David every day of His life, and this service kept him dining in God's house for the rest of his life *(see Psalm 23)*.

The answer to your strength is God. Whatever you are facing, whatever you struggle with, whatever is weighing you down, rest in his loving arms. God never lets the righteous fall (*Psalm 55:22*).

What God Gives You Is Your Own

Your grace is yours. No one can move you and stand in your space to usurp your blessings because as they try to push you by whatever means, your grace moves with you. Focus your heart on thanking God for what He gives you. Such a state and condition fill your heart with gladness. You cannot want a more fantastic plan. It is yours, use it!

It is by God's grace that you have been saved through faith. For it is by God's grace that your efforts are accepted as gifts to him. It is not the result of your own *(Ephesians 2:8-9)*.

Here is what the wise man Solomon says concerning his happiness with his lot *"...this is a gift from God. He seldom reflects on the days of his life, because God keeps him occupied with gladness of heart"* (Eccles. 5:19b–20).

God Alone Must be in the Driver's Seat

Jesus proclaimed, *"I am the way, the truth, and the life..." (John 14:6).* You want no perfect driver than Him. The success of the mission and journey depends upon who is in the driver's seat. John advised that Jesus is the bread of life. Anyone who goes to Him will never be hungry, and all who believe in Him will never be thirsty *(John 6:35).*

The responsibility to stay filled and thoroughly quenched depends on every individual. You have to believe the verse and believe God that you will never want anything while you are in Him. God instructs that He alone supplies the needs of His children.

Life's supplies are available for you. Let go of the control of your life. Put God in control, let Him guide, direct, and supply all, and all will be well.

"Be persuaded that neither death, with its voice of fear, nor life with its many fears, nor the attack of the enemy which falsely accuse you, nor things present with their pressuring claims, nor things to come with their dark shadows, nor the height of any mountain that stand in your way, nor the depths of a great trial that you may walk through, nor any person or circumstance which tries to quench your joy or rob you of your peace shall be able to move you away by even a single inch, from the love of God which covers and guards your life" (Roy Lessin, March 24, 2011).

Agree On Finances

One of the leading causes of friction in marriage is the lack of efficient money management and the inability of the couple to handle the family income wisely. This problem often leads to divorce. To use the family finances wisely, the husband and the wife must each understand their responsibilities within the framework of a budget mutually agreed

Spend some valuable time and prepare a detailed budget outlining the responsibilities you will each have for your finances. You will find how practical and beneficial this financial guide is for the marriage.

"Most people think to allow making, spending or investing money a goodly part of their precious time. It should, therefore, be of no surprise to learn that money is also one of the key factors in producing a happy or an unhappy marriage. However, you may be surprised to learn that it is rarely the lack of adequate financial resources that destroy the happiness of a marriage. It is the couple's attitude toward material things." (Thomas and Thomas "Beginning Your Marriage," Eighth Edition, ACTA Publication, Chicago, Illinois, p.149).

"Your devotional life as a couple is no substitute for your personal relationship with Christ."

The couple's attitude towards material things such as cars, houses, lands, stocks, insurance, credit cards, TV, radios, and other desires can become a power issue, more than the money issue itself, which can wreak havoc on a marriage. Usually, one's attitude towards money depends on what they adopted from their parents. If money signifies security for a "free sailing" life - to shop, travel, or be adventurous, this financial behavior will continue in the marriage.

Facing Economic Future

Because of the economic situation faced by everyone today, it is expected that both husband and wife should be employed. Such a way of life has become scenario has the norm; however, it is for the husband and wife to agree on the way forward depending on their particular circumstance. This couple should never allow the economic situation to hinder the well-being of the marriage.

Many influences make a person either positive or negative. Habits, relationships, experiences have significantly impacted one's life. One's attitude towards money faces the same fate. They should never allow the difficulty that money causes to interfere with the progress of the marriage.

Money matters in the marriage. Whatever one may have experienced in their home with money, within the marriage, the use of money takes on a whole new dimension. The husband and wife are now personally responsible for the financial operation of their home. They should have full knowledge of all their financial obligations and budget accordingly. They should be honest with each other and with the situation for the smooth operation of the marriage.

It is difficult enough to begin a new life and add to the stresses that poor money management may cause. *Good money management in a marriage can be a very loving thing (Thomas and Thomas p157).*

Having discussed finance and its importance, we would agree that money plays a significant role in life as a whole. Money is not an essential commodity for the comfort and welfare of every individual. It is how others are helped to experience a comfortable life as well. However, once it is not idolized, it should bring good to its recipients.

Fear Not

Even with a proper financial guideline like a budget, you will face hardships. Be reminded: have no fear; God is with you. Do not be dismayed; He is your God. He promised to strengthen and uphold you with His righteous right hand (*Isaiah 4:10*).

Stressful financial conditions like losing a job, serious health problems, and rebellious children, will press in to demand your attention and energy. Sometimes these hardships and stresses are so tricky that friends and family members cannot help to fix them. Yes, they may empathize and genuinely care but honestly cannot do anything.

Being alone then can make you feel that all is lost. You are not! God's presence is constant. His strength is always present. His promise is true. He will hold you up. He will strengthen you, and He will lead you through it. You are never out of God's reach.

God's Blessings Know No End

God's blessing begins with His call. Abraham and Sarah experienced it, and so did Isaac and Rebekah. You will never live one second without God's enabling grace.

Moses coined it nicely for you, *"The Lord Jesus bless you and keep you; the Lord make His face shine upon you and be gracious to you; the Lord turn His face toward you and give you peace" (Numbers 6:24-26).*

God's blessings call for a response in your life. You have to walk towards Him at all times. His peace lies in the very path you are traveling. God's face turns towards you, so He sees any chaos that is creeping up along the way.

The excellent assurance you have in all this is the confidence that God's place does not change. Do not move your focus away from Him. God's peace is forever.

Your Relationship With God Counts

No one places confidence in someone he does not know. As one comes to know God and the relationship grows, there is a world of difference for life ahead.

How would the relationship grow? How would the walk have meaning? Such confidence is derived from reading daily the Word of God. God speaks through His word. There in scripture, He reveals His character, His love, direction, and desired obedience. You "respond to God by promising Him your fidelity and obedience in return" *(Martin L Smith, "Reconciliation for Confession in the Episcopal Church." Phillip Turner, "Sex Money and Power" Cambridge, Mass., 1985 p. 20).*

If you want Christ to spend time with you, you have to spend time with Him in prayer, meditation, and in His word. In this manner, you will understand His love which He declares, passes all human comprehension.

Maintain Your Own Personal Walk With God

Your walk with Christ keeps you aware that strength comes not from you but from God. Personal Bible Study and Prayer are the salts that keep your spirituality awakened.

Be mindful that the best thing you can give your spouse is yourself; then, the second gift should be a life walking strong with the Lord. Your holy life as a couple is no substitute for your relationship with Christ. Continue to sharpen your workings with your Saviour and Redeemer. You not only would be awed by His holiness, but you will be thrilled over the quality of your marriage.

God who formed you before you came to the belly wants to maintain a relationship with you. This is the reason why He remarked to Jeremiah, *"Before I formed you in the womb, I knew you before you were born I set you apart…." (Jer. 1:5 GNB).*

The word 'apart' is significant. It means you are mine forever. What a powerful message! Our God knows each of us before we was formed in the womb. He placed us aside as unique only to Him for His plans.

No one came into this world by accident. Everyone came through God's energy for His purpose; that is, for His specific gifts. Each of us has our ability, and each of us is loved by God to perform our God's duty. You have Christ's imprint on your life.

STAYING CONNECTED

The Connection Is Not Seen

The true Christian never sees the connection to Christ. The occupants are either using lamps, candles, or other mechanical devices to provide light in some homes. Different homes have electrical wires led from the pole, but the electrical power is not seen.

One's relationship with the Lord is very much like the house that is powered by electrical current that lights the home. This is the electricity that enables others to feel the effect of a current life that runs through them from Christ.

For this reason, a man shall leave his father and mother and be united with his wife, and the two shall be one flesh." "This is a profound mystery," says Paul. Someone once said, *"1+1 = 1."* This is what the marriage bond is.

Users of Christ's current brings to others Christ's character, attributes, awesomeness, compassion, and love. It is the seed that makes others bear fruits and is drawn closer to Him to experience how wonderful He is.

Keep The Connection Buttons And Lines Clear

He was keeping connecting buttons and lines clear calls for maintaining an understanding of God's word. As God's word is learned, it is then returned to Him in prayer. God opens His children's hearts to the possibilities of knowing Him by observing His word in them.

Enjoy a prayer life filled only with God's word giving to Him.
The conversation gives and taken...statement, response; listening, question, answer, statement, agreement, question, disagreement, information, response—listening, listening, listening, comment, reply,

comment. There must be attention; there must be hearing...talk all the time to each other. This keeps the conversation button on and the line clear *(Premarital Guidance, Dick Rossie BD DD Litt 1963 pgs. 44-45)*.

The apostle Paul advises, *"Christ's message in all its richness must live in your hearts. Teach and instruct one another with all wisdom. Sing Psalms, Hymns, and sacred songs. Sing to God with thanksgiving in your heart"* *(Col. 3:16)*.

Find Contentment In The Marriage

Be happy with your wife and find joy with the woman you love. Pretty and graceful as a deer. Let her charms keep you satisfied. Let her reward you with her love (Proverbs 5:18). Contentment or peace of mind with satisfaction only resides when both the husband and wife find their abiding place in their Lord and Saviour, Jesus Christ. Where they come from, their friend, where they live, their job, leisure, play, and the like do not bring contentment. Today's world puts much importance on money. The more money one has, the more successful one is perceived to be.

Many books and articles are written giving ideas about getting more money and spending what you have. The enticing point in all this is to make money the number one priority of your life, with all the other preferences growing from that one. But some things are much more important than money. God and

"Step back and remember how God has blessed your marriage and how He cares for you."

all His attributes – wisdom and understanding gained through His Word will have a more profound impact on what kind of persons the husband and wife are and will ultimately impact the marriage. This will leave a more lasting legacy with friends, family, and enemies alike than the knowledge that Mack and Maisie were wealthy, possessing all amenities of life, yet there was very little happiness.

We are reminded to *"get wisdom, it is worth more than money;"* choose insight over income every time *(Proverbs 16:16)*. Paul advises, *"Little is much when God is in it,"* while the writer of Proverbs admonishes, *"It is far better to be right and poor than to be wrong and rich" (Proverbs 16:8)*.

Celebrate Occasions Together

Share your Partner's happiness. Right from the start, set out to keep your relationship alive. Do not ever get too busy with each other. Phone or call if you are apart. An unexpected gift, however small, will keep your romance alive. (Getting Married, Family Doctor Publication. Published by British Medical Association. 1977. P18). It will be joy without measure. Graduation, weddings, birthdays, vacation, promotions, retirement, good times with friends, going to church, and good health is events in a couple's lives that should be celebrated together. It may be an anniversary and or recovery; make the celebration heavenly sprinkled with laughter. Do all in your power to keep the conversations animated, light hearted, and filled with happy memories. God is always pleased to see a couple enjoying themselves so much.

As you sit around the dinner table, let your conversation flow. Share memories. Create an atmosphere of love; it will keep the heart of each other stirred and declare to the world how much you enjoy each other.

Each partner must do their best to be pleasant to be around. God fills lives with good qualities to keep you in a bond. God will help you be considerate of others, especially the love of your life.

Life is not meant to be lived alone. God put us on His earth to live in the community. He puts it thus: *"Be fruitful and replenish the earth" (Gen 1:28)*. So He is pleased when we live in a community with friends and family.

God intends that we encourage one another. In tough times we can promote the other. When your faith wants to wane, another's faith can stimulate yours until you find spiritual standing again.

As you and your wife walk side by side, your faith is genuine and strong. Do not try to journey alone; let the other assist you. The apostle Paul has a word, *"I long to see you so that I may impart to you some spirited gift to make you strong in that you and I may be mutually encouraged by each other's faith" (Romans 1:11-12).*

Do not try to go it alone. Let your husband/wife encourage you.

Keep The Marriage Intact

The wise man Solomon says, *"She brings him good, not harm, all the days of her life" (Proverbs 31:12).* This saying is for both the husband and the wife to do to each other.

Get busy with the housework, attending to the children, your job, meetings for the children, your Church, and the list goes on, making you feel that there are not enough hours in the day. But remember! Your marriage relationship is essential. Spend time with each other. Leave some energy for conversation and other essential things with each other.

The priorities must be established from day one, and they are to be maintained. Give your marriage relationship the ample time it deserves. Give each other the time and energy each deserves. Bring good to each other to show how important the other is to you.

God Will Protect You: Protect One Another

Married couples are to be a hiding place for each other. The burdens of life weigh down on the marriage, and sometimes there seems to be no relief; do not run away and hide. No matter how long you hide, the problem will still be there. The safe place to find refuge is in the available space of each other. *"He will keep you safe from all hidden dangers. He will cover you with His wings; you will be safe in His love. His faithfulness will protect and defend you" (Psalm 91:3-4 GNB).*

Sure enough, the couple that gives God His rightful place is protected, for He is available to be a safe place, a protected place, and a hiding place. The hymn writer puts it this way, *"Hiding in Thee, Hiding in Thee, Thou blest Rock of Ages, I am hiding in Thee"* (Cushing, 282). God is available for those who trust in Him. The word trust is an exciting element of life because it means believing God is there and that He is working around the clock, even while one cannot see Him doing so. Trust Him to take care of the marriage, trust Him to take care of you and your spouse; only then will He indeed be your refuge.

With these precautions, who can be discouraged? Who can get down-spirited? Hardship only arises in the eyes of the husband and the wife if one or the other is not contented with what they have.

If friends become the spotlight, if there is jealousy as to what others possess, such as the big house, the newest brand and the latest style of car, an impressive career, or the success of a child or children, then your wants become more crystallized and discouraging steps

Marriage partners need a heart of contentment. By all means, grow bigger and better but in stride while God supplies your needs according to His favor, and do not envy others.

Being at peace assists growth, improvement, and achievement. Therefore be at peace and defeat discouragement. It is a condition that soothes the heart rather than frantically running around trying to grab more than your share out of life.

In discouragement, we sometimes get stuck with blinkers at the side of our eyes. All that lies in the fore are things that are wrong for our lives. We know we do not have the power to get the things we are longing for, yet we are still grabbing.

> *"...a cheerful look brings joy to the heart and good news gives health to the bone."*

Let your eyes be focused and clear so that you can see what God has in store for you. Grasp the immensity of the glorious way of life God has for his followers. He has an utter abundance of his work for those who trust Him. He has available endless energy and boundless strength.

God crowns us with love and mercy. He gives us a paradise crown, and wraps us in goodness, and gives us beauty eternal. He renews breath and keeps young all who are in His presence.

Bearing in mind the kind of God we have, do not be disappointed when God does not act. If we make our plans for life and ask Him to bless them, do not become discouraged when He does not do what we want Him to do. Yes, God does great things for us every day; He forgives our sins, He forgets not all His benefits; God heals all our diseases and crowns with love and compassion, He satisfies our desires with good things and saves us from the pit of hell. God wants the husband and the wife to give up on consumerism and hostility toward their differences and practice generous and forgiving grace. (Miroslav Volf Unconditional, Charisma House, 2010 P xviii.)

God was with Israel for forty years, and the writer of Deuteronomy wrote, *"God, our God has blessed you in everything you have done. He has guarded you in your travel through this immense wilderness. For forty years now, God, your God has been right here with you, you should not lack one thing, says Moses"* (Deut. 2:7).

The Hebrew people had a habit of quickly forgetting God's work among them, and they slid back into their pattern of complaining about their situation. So Moses wrote and helped them to focus on God's goodness and care.

Moses' remedy is the right recipe when a marriage is struggling with life. Step back and remember how God has blessed your wedding and how He cares for you. God has not let you lack one thing. Hold on to what you have and move forward, trusting only Him.

Put more confidence in the hands of your Maker, the one Christ Jesus. Matthew the Evangelist makes the point, *"You tired, worn out, burned out, turn to God, and you will recover your life"* (Matt. 11:28, The Scribe). God is standing beside you at this moment. His arms are outstretched, beckoning you to come to Him. If you close your eyes and walk to Him, you will find each step you take, the burden on your shoulder becomes lighter.

Jesus makes a unique appeal to those who are worn out from carrying heavyweight. He knows that we all need what He has to offer. Take the first step for the good of your marriage. Perhaps you are the one He is calling. Step right into His circle. The promise of rest is pretty enticing. Let go of self, pride, and ego. Go to Him. You will never regret what you did.

God gives a hand to those down on their luck, and He provides a fresh start to those who are ready to quit *(Ps. 145:14)*. Relatives and friends may empathize for a moment, but if you take the matter to God and stay quiet before Him, waiting for what you need, you will find what you are looking for.

There is no other who will lift you. God may not take your problems away, but He will walk you through them. Satan's angels did have a go at Paul, but Paul got on his knees and sought God three times for relief. God's response was, *"My grace is enough; it is all you need. My strength comes into its own in your weakness" (2 Cor. 12:9)*. Go to God! Whatever betide, He will take care of you.

You Have Chosen Your Partner Now Choose Your Path

"For this reason, a man will leave his father and mother and unite with his wife, and the two will become one" (Matt 19:5 GNB). You are on your way to success if you choose Christ's way. After the agreement and the church's blessing, God takes up His rightful place in the marriage. He is prepared to lead each individual along the way. Wherever God carries you, go. As you travel alone, know that He is there every step of the way.

If the journey seems impossible, remember how impossible it was for Joseph, whose wife was pregnant with Jesus, God's son. When Moses got to the Red Sea, he saw no road, yet God said to him, take my people to the promised land. It was Pharaoh who spoke to Moses, take your people and go.

The choice to climb down or up is yours. You are free to choose the direction of your new life. You can choose to follow those who try to influence you to live life outside of the circle of obedience to God because they care nothing about Him or His values. Or you can take God at His Word and be successful.

God's law is the accepted way. Jesus instructed from the beginning what God's intended will was to be *(Matt 19:8)*.

The couple in marriage should choose to surround themselves with friends who will encourage one another along the road and hold you accountable in your walk with Christ.

Do Not Be Hard-Headed And Stubborn

The husband and wife must work together by appreciating what each brings to the table for the unity of the marriage (Scot McKnight From Wheaton To Rome: Evangelicals Become Roman Catholic Journal of the Evangelical Theological Society, P468). Do not be at odds day in and day out. Do not shut off your communication with each other. Do not give each other the cold shoulder. Your life is too short, and your marriage life is too precious to live a life that way. It is always possible to make it right with your husband or wife while still having the opportunity.

I know of a couple who had a vehement difference of opinion one night. They slept in the same bed, but her head was at his feet, and his head was at her feet. In the morning, they left the house still not speaking to each other. Later that day, she got the news that her husband passed in an accident. That woman is still living with the emotional pain.

Is Sex Confined To The Bedroom?

Sex draws its meaning from the whole life of love between husband and wife. Many husbands would testify that their sexual lovemaking began while the couple was preparing dinner in the kitchen, sitting in the living room, or bathing. However, each spouse has their sexual preference as to where, when, and how. Often they should make love. Understanding and cooperation are vital concerning each other's likes and dislikes. No recipe book prescribes that sex is only confined to the bedroom.

MEETING EACH OTHER'S
EMOTIONAL NEEDS
♥ ♥ ♥

Keep The Relationship Very Warm

You are reminded by the wise man Solomon that they will keep warm when two lie down together. One cannot stay warm alone *(Eccles. 4:11).*

It is a delight to be cold and experience the warmth of someone's arms around your shoulders.

"A cord of three strands is harder to pop (Eccles. 4:12). The third person in this instance is God."

When you are worried, another person's companionship is a cup of cold water on a scorching and humid day. The "ups and downs" of life will make you feel cold. This is the time you will need the warmth of each other. In times like these, it does you no good to be alone.

Your good times are more pleasant as you share them. These times deepen your memories and enhance the relationship. Such a condition will help you through tricky times emotionally and spiritually. Be there for each other. It does all the good to require one another.

Keep Up What You Began

Remember the feelings you experienced at the beginning of your relationship? You never had enough of each other; you never did enough for each other; you always wanted to see each other and be in each other's company. You continually showed each other how much you cared.

What caused the difference now? Do you speak the exact words to each other? Do you still send love notes? Is your priority still to have each other as your best friend? When you speak to each other, is there a glow from your face?

If you are not answering every question positively, it means that there are hidden agendas. It means that your thoughts, words, and deeds are not motivated by love. You have forgotten the "always" with which you promised to love.

A Cheerful Look Keeps The Marriage Glowing

It is advisable to take scripture seriously. Proverbs instruct that a cheerful look brings joy to the heart and good news gives health to the bone.

The same book of Proverbs instructs that the woman sets the atmosphere in the home. The wife/mother keeps an eye on everyone in her household and keeps them all busy and productive. Her children respect and bless her; her husband joins in with words of praise *(Proverbs 31:28)*.

The mother keeps the momentum of the family going by the way she handles life and reacts to problems. The tone of joy is set, and how God works in situations is demonstrated because everyone in the household is happy. Here, faith finds its place in the home. God is trusted when signs of His work are being acted out in real experiences of life

Communication

I see him every day. I see her every day. What is there to talk over? Talk every morning as to what you hope to accomplish during the day. Talk every night as to what your successes and failures were. What were your anxious moments? What were your worst fears?

"Each partner deserves the best treatment, the most patience, love and understanding the other can give.

You are to grasp the opportunity to energize each other every single day. "I know you can do it." "Stick with it; the end will surprise you." "Whatever the outcome,

I am here for you; we will talk it over." Communication is the fuel that causes the engine to run through the challenges life presents.

It is always better when husband and wife listen to each other. This method of communication encourages each other. All that is necessary is to spend time and energy communicating to encourage each other every day (*see Hebrews 3:13*).

Do not talk to your parents about the things you should be discussing with your spouse. You have created new avenues of communication, and that is with your spouse. You should establish that new loyalty and responsibility with each other and not your parents.

Your parents' opinion may not be your spouse's. However, you should learn from the wisdom of your parents when making decisions together as husband and wife. Mom and Dad's way of dealing with situations may be different, although helpful. With communication, you can work out your difficulties together.

There is a reason why you have been blessed as a couple. You have placed your hands in God's hands. You have trusted Him to direct your path, guide you through, and be used by Him in many ways.

God's fragrance is all over you. It will precede you as you travel each day. Others will know you are on your way even before they see you. Even when you have passed miles away, all will know that God is in your midst by the fragrance you leave behind.

The saved and the unsaved marriage will want what you have - the aroma of Christ. God will lead you in every process because you make yourself available for Him to guide you.

St. Paul thanked God for being there to lead His children through difficulties. So they can spread The fragrance of Christ (*see 2 Cor. 2:14-15*).

Submit Yourselves To Each Other

This submission means no reservation of sharing one to the other because submission in the marriage is a covenant. A covenant is an ancient formal contract between two parties involving mutual obligations sealed under oath (*Bruce Feiler, "Abraham" 2004 Harper College publishers, pg. 39*). You love each other and want the best for each other and your marriage.

Each day, you seek to be examples of God's love to those around you, especially your children, relatives, and friends.

Your submission amounts to each not seeking their way but endeavoring to build the other up, especially in the presence of everyone else.

Do not strive to be indifferent, especially in the area where one is more qualified and has a better understanding of the situation. Work as a lever and make your house a home, your marriage a life experience, and your ministry the best you can for others to copy.

Body Partners

The apostle Paul gives us a great picture when he described believers as being parts of Christ's body! All the body parts differ, but they have the same concern for one another. "If one part ...is praised all the other parts share its happiness" *(1 Cor. 12:25)*.

As with a human body, each partner in the marriage has a part to play. No one else can contribute what God has willed for you both within the marriage bond.

Understand that each one must serve with his life as a gift to the other. It is only in that manner will your marriage receive the contribution intended. When you have made your contribution, watch the positive response,

"Each day in the marriage should be lived ... to rediscover the joy the relationship began with for a healthier outlook on life."

56

and your mind will be filled with satisfaction for what you (with God's help) have done for a healthy marriage.

Your prize will be shared with you both. God is using you in this form to work with each other for the common good of His body. The Church. Your celebration means that God's work is being done so well in your marriage, a part of Christ's body.

Individually, it would help if you rejoiced to see the unique place and the great responsibility you have taken on for the betterment of the body of Christ, while at the same time you are filling in with everyone else as a unit responding to Christ, your head.

God said, *"It is not good for the man to be alone; I will make him a helper suitable for him" (Gen 2:18).*

This is a true revelation of God's desire for man to live in unity (relationships) with one another. Helper, in this case, was never intended to be a servant in the menial sense. God never intended that office to belong to a lesser being with whom a man will find to share his life.

A husband and a wife share a fantastic relationship. As best friends, they share hopes, fears, dreams, worries, service, space, all to build each other to be the best of their kind, serving their creator side by side.

The statement "behind every good man is a good woman" is unkind and derogatory information. From the beginning, God intended the information to be "beside every good man is a good woman." The opposite is also true "beside every good woman is a good man."

"When there is a harsh word, lend a deaf ear, switch to a lower gear and take the vehicle off the bumpy terrain."

Genesis reminds us that it was God who established a community of people in His world. This established relationship then declares that man is never alone in the world. It was Adam, Eve, and God. Today, you, your spouse and God, and by extension, the persons who are your neighbors.

When you, your spouse, and God share in the community, life is better than when it is not shared. Life is undoubtedly much better when it is shared with someone. When life's challenges strike you down, you are helpless in pulling yourself up. When another is with you, you will be encouraged and even be pulled up to try again.

Here is what wisdom dictates if one is overpowered - two can protect themselves. A cord of three strands is more brutal to pop, said the wise man Soloman *(Eccles. 4:12).* The third person in this instance is God. His presence daily is a must for a successful marriage relationship. As You fall in love with Him daily, do the same with each other. "A successful marriage requires falling ihttps://www.supanet.com/find/famous-quotes-by/pope-john-paul- love many times, always with the same person" (Pope John Paul 11 on Marriage—Famous Quotes-Supanet).

Be Close To Each Other

Here are some suggestions for maintaining a closer relationship with your spouse:

- Embrace
- Walk hand in hand
- Use your time together to focus on each other
- Find time to laugh at each other and with each other
- Invite the other out for a special meal
- Go for moonlight walks
- Set dates and keep them
- Create the atmosphere for suggestions or guidance in making decisions
- Seek time alone without the radio, television, or the children
- Be affectionate without it always ending in sex
- Play your part to make the time together meaningful
- Show appreciation for each other and your time together
- Thank God for each other

RESOLVING CONFLICT

♥ ♥ ♥

Be Patient With Each Other

Give each other credit for all that is done. Each partner deserves to be loved and respected *(see Proverbs 31:31)*. Most often than not, marriage partners have less patience with each other than with others. Best behaviors are displayed on the outside. In the home, tolerance is replaced by a fuse that cuts out more often than not. Hence patience, communication, and understanding are still on their journey home and are not in any hurry to arrive.

IN A marriage the husband, always speaks of his intelligence, his accolades, and successes. His wife, who was gifted in her talent but less intelligent, bossed her around. All over her over with words, just to let her know she was inferior. In achievement than he. The woman, ashamed and embarrassed, mustered these words, *"I know that I am beneath you in achievements; however, if anything happens to you, I will with patience look after you."* Not long after, the husband fell ill with a severe sickness. The wife's words came to pass. She stayed with him through *"the thick and thin."* Patience is not only for the state of being; it is for the realities of life.

Each partner deserves the best treatment, the most patience, love, and understanding the other can give. Paul wrote to the people of Thessalonica and advised them to be patient with each other *(I Thess. 5:14)*.

Do not let your words tumble out; they hurt, take away worth, and diminish self-esteem. Then life takes a downward turn because of such behavior.

Be Compassionate

God's compassion for Israel was demonstrated when He said, *"I have seen the affliction of my people who are in Egypt and have heard their cry because of their task-masters. I know their sufferings, and I have come down to deliver them..." (Exodus 3:7-8).* In Hosea 11:8, God reiterated His compassion for Israel when He said, *"my heart recoils within me, my compassion grows warm and tender."* And Jesus on the cross showed the same compassion when at His death He poured out His mercy on His offenders *"Father, forgive them, for they know not what they do" (Luke 23:37).* Each partner needs to look at what kind of temper is exhibited. Is frustration hoarded, then exploded over a straw? How do you react when you become upset? Do you take time to react to situations with genuine composure?

It is always good to ask oneself how Christ would react in this given situation. What will be His reaction if I make this decision without His intervention? How would my other half feel? How will my husband/wife react? Will this decision bring about peace? Remember to make a compassionate decision – do it in love. The Psalmist reminds us that *"God is all mercy and grace – not quick to anger, is rich in love" (Ps. 145:8).*

Be In A Constant State Of Forgiveness

"Do to others as you would want them to do for you" (Matt 7:12). Be willing to forgive seventy times seven daily. It is not godly to ask for something you are not willing to give. Jesus' prayer teaches this. It speaks of God's forgiveness daily.

It makes no sense to ask God for the forgiveness of one's sins if we are not willing to forgive others who have wronged us. Eventually, your world will become very small, and you might run out of space to operate. You will cease to touch lives, and you will have no one as a working companion.

In life, you will wrong someone, and someone will wrong you - such is the way of life. If you share the wrong that others do to you, it will grow into hatred and become an enemy of God. If you want God's forgiveness, you have to "show the same grace" to others as you want God to show to you.

We ought to calm our hearts, minds, and souls and forgive others before we seek forgiveness before God, to be ignored by our impaired relationship with Him. While we are on our knees with our face to the rising sun, the unforgiveness exercised by us sticks out like a sore thumb with a bandage and needs healing before the petition.

Be A Sincere Couple

"My darling, when compared with other young women, you are a lily among thorns" (Song of Songs 2:2). There must not be any acting but be over doers with love and show concern for each other. It does not take long for one who is genuine to realize when one is insincere. Yes! When sincerity is lacking the arms of the different folds.

If you are not in love with someone, do not move into marriage. You cannot find lasting happiness with one as a partner. The property will not fill the void. It takes a love that never gives up, cares more for others than for oneself, does not crave for what it does not have, and is not puffed up. Such love does not force itself on others. A Love that is not pushy, believing in 'me first,' that does not fly off the handle, that never keeps the score of the wrongs against others. Still, but delights in the humble truth, which trusts God continually, look forward rather than looking backward, and finds the best in others to keep the marriage relationship going to the end.

When sincerity is present in the above types of love, its dividends are drawn daily. It will be believable and will draw others into its orbit.

It was genuine love that kept David's and Jonathan's hearts fixed in a relationship as terrific friends. King Saul, Jonathan's father, did not like David, but Saul's attitude did not make Jonathan's friendship with David any less sincere.

Jonathan had every right to follow in his father's footsteps and hate David; after all, he was the rightful heir to Saul's throne. However, Jonathan realized that David was God's choice for that throne, and all things being considered, they accepted what was best for the relationship and remained friends unto death *(see 1 Sam. 18:4ff)*.

Sincerity gives a chance for the potential to become a reality. So give sobriety its rightful place. The success of the marriage depends upon it.

Negativity Breeds Negativity

The spirit of broken cake is a sign of negativity. If one stops and stares at the broken cake, the invitation of a dark cloud's presence takes place; eventually, that cloud gets blacker and blacker, and everything then looks dismal.

Negativity generally sees a glass half empty instead of half full. Where negativity finds its seat, the arena is not fun. The people engaged in the play get into a negative cycle which is extremely hard to avoid.

Anyone who lives in the cycle of negativity sees everything as evil; every situation is complex and does not see much hope; remember, the glass is half empty for that person. However, the person who sees the glass half full makes an effort to see things positively. Thanks are offered for the glass half full for it is better than starting at the bottom. The remaining stairs are climbed with much enthusiasm to the top of the glass to make it complete.

Each day in the marriage should be lived with all the fibers of the couple's being to rediscover the relationship's joy with a healthier outlook on life.

Married life is strong as long as the parties involved have a positive mindset. God has allowed the relationship of which He took residence to glow. The couple thus far has continued faith in God and faith in each other. The way forward depends on the continued dedication and the steadfast look at achieving goals and providing stimulus for increased confidence and endurance.

Positive relationships should not stop growing. At this point, all parties should look at the top of that tree. This calls for unlimited love, trust and commitment; remember, the glass is half full, not half empty. Married life is never in the category of polite relationships; far from it, this is real love-ship, this is forever. This relationship is a real love affair; it is built upon Christ's foundation. That foundation is what both parties are required to share.

Be Obedient At All Times

Every marriage has its crises. Your marriage is not the only one with problems. Do not beat yourself up; slowly, working with God, and you will find the solution. Remember one thing, you just have to go to God with all your cares, and He will lead you over the mound. *"Only be thou strong and very courageous that thou mayest observe to do according to all the law which Moses, my servant, commanded thee turn not from it to the right hand or the left that thou mayest prosper wherever you go" (Joshua 1:7).*

Carolyn Larsen advises that *"Discouragement makes you focus on the moment. You get stuck on the pain, the hopelessness or the loneliness in your heart" (Larsen, One Minute Devotions for Women, May 17).*

God who dwells in the obedient heart will give you hope in the place of hopelessness, joy instead of loneliness because He cares when you are hurting and will do all to keep you committed to make it.

The Psalmist declares that God *"Rescues the poor who call to Him and those who are needy and neglected. He pities the weak and poor; He saves the lives of those in need. He rescues them from oppression and violence; their lives are precious to Him" (Psalm 72:12-14).*

Yancey advises Christians that *"God promises a safe landing but not necessarily a calm passage" (Philip D Yancey)*. Do not be discouraged on the trip. Pain, stress, and trials of all sorts will lie in the path to make the journey bumpy. Do not cave in, or you will be defeated. Persevere, keep your anchor up and the chain tightly fastened, remember, you have not reached the harbor; it is only a hump in the road.

The Psalmist David wrote encouraging words as he hid beneath the cave from those who wanted to kill him. When you read these words, you will be spellbound; He said, *"When I am ready to give up, He knows what I shall do. In the path where I walk, my enemies have hidden a trap for me" (Psalm 142:3)*. In the cave, David remembered that God was in control.

King Saul had no good reason to hunt down David. David had done nothing wrong to the king. David was God's choice, and being so chosen, King Saul hated him and was determined to kill him.

David had no desire to retaliate. He had opportunities to get rid of Saul once and for all, 1 Sam. 23: 14—24; 24. but alas! He was God's awaited King of Israel. He failed to become angry with God. He trusted God, knowing fully that his problems and their answers are in the hands of God. Think about this!

Be Gentle With Each Other

Sometimes you may feel that the other person just does not "get it." No matter how you explain, the other person just does not understand. The situation does not call for raising your voice or answering in a harsh tone. Such response results in a downhill ride that become rougher and rougher as the path opens up.

There is a trick to stopping the downhill spiral. When there is a harsh word, lend a deaf ear, switch to a lower gear and take the vehicle off the bumpy terrain. When you are about to lose your grip or cool, bring the ship to a stop, take deep breaths and speak gently. You stand to gain, and you will be the better for it. *"Although you are imperfect, the Lord can use you still if you confess your sins to Him and seek to do His will" (Spar).*

God Will Quiet You With His Love

The prophet Zephaniah saw God's presence at all times in the life of His children, so he assured: *"The Lord your God is with you. He is mighty to save, God will take great care of you; Hi swill quiet you in His love, He will rejoice over you with His singing" (Zephaniah 3:17).*

When you feel alone in the middle of a journey, do not struggle with life's problems. God is there to fight the battle. Stand back, give first place to Him; his thoughts and mind are pure to answer whatever is untoward.

This situation serves to test your maturity. As you are so tested, remember it is a natural process because your marriage is a test of your devotion to Christ. *(Dr. Emerson Eggerichs; "Love & Respect Thomas Nelson 2004 p .295).*

No one else can settle or quiet you but God. Do not wish that you were not there or that you would fly away from that spot. When your heart beats frantically and has shortness of breath, listen for His heartbeat over yours, saying I am in control.

The Wrong Way Of Life Can Never Win

The Psalmist was right when he admonished, "Fret not yourself because of evildoers or be envious of those who do wrong; for like the grass they will soon wither, like green plants they will soon die away" (Psalm 37:1-2).

It is not a second-best relationship. Enter the relationship with enthusiasm, knowing that the woman or man is for you. Do not enter your marriage with a second-best, or because no one else with better credentials is available; and so, hoping that the relationship will work *(Russell l Dicks, "Premarital Guidance" Prentice-Hall 1963, p .91).*

Try tenderness; it nurtures growth and maturity, sending its roots deep down into understanding. So when your will is frustrated, you will seek to share your feelings and strengthen your relationship through difficulties. Remember, "the mature person can accept responsibility, make decisions and abide by them without harming the others directly involved in the relationship" *(Dicks p. 90).*

"...Sharpen each other with gentleness, kind attitudes and loving words."

Sometimes it seems that the bad things of life are winning! Around you, the condition of our world speaks that way: wars, poverty, domestic violence, church splits, child abuse, the rich get richer while the poor get poorer, and the list goes on and on. Does one wonder where it is God?

Christians are to keep on trusting God. The bad of life will always get its due one day. God will prevail! God's offer stands, and it is only won at the end of the journey, so stick around. He who wins on earth may not necessarily succeed in eternity if God is not their source.

Injustice In A Marriage

When speaking of suffering injustice, it must be remembered that no one is entirely innocent or immune. However, each individual should be free to make decisions, have their own space, make their friends, and be entitled to their own opinion. (Dicks p 83). There are many times when hostility in a relationship may lead to hurtful words, and events have sprung from mutual disrespect. Both sides have made their contribution to the injustice. What will end the cycle of injustice with its revengeful behavior is forgiveness. This attitude enables the husband and wife to forget the hurt and move forward together beyond remembering the pitfalls. Brian Zahard declares, "To live well, there are things to remember, and there are things to forget." *(Zahard, Unconditional Library of Congress Cataloging in Publication Data (USA) p. 67).*

Never Possess A Negative Attitude

A negative attitude feeds self. This brings pain and alienation in the marriage. An examination is necessary on both husband and wife to be sure that neither is the problem. It is said, "Some people do not have a problem, they are the problem" *(Howard Clinebell, Basic Types of Pastoral Care Counselling," Resources for the Ministry of Healing and Growth, [Revised and enlarged] Abingdon Press p. 153).* Sometimes women may say, "When my husband starts doing what I ask him to do, then we will get along as a married couple should, and we will have peace," or "If my husband starts picking up his stuff, then I'll quit being so nagging." Or the man may say, "When my wife starts putting my meals on the table, then we will get along fine," or "I will be a better person and stop being rude to my spouse when she starts treating me right."

Marriages with such self-esteem need to undergo spiritual surgery to remove the ego and be plastered with humility. Failing this operation, Items that are allowed to sore and fester will cause spouses to be at each other's throats. Surely they may love each other deep within, but allowing strife to take a prominent place drives wedges into the relationship over the years.

A House Divided Will Be Destroyed

Jesus said, "A constantly squabbling family falls to pieces." *(The Message, The Bible in Contemporary Language, Numbered edition; Luke 11:17).* Yes! If you allow fights and quarrels into your relationship, that relationship will be brought to destruction.

I am not talking about overnight destruction. It may not be a couple of months or even a few years. If you allow grudges, sarcastic remarks, and such like to control you, you destroy the relationship. "Be quick to recognize the good qualities in each other" *(Ellen G White, Adventist Home, p.107).*

When Difficulty Strikes

"take a hard look at yourself. You might be amazed to discover that your own hard-hearted, inconsiderate attitude is the real cause of your marital unhappiness" *(Edmeade, James (1994). Before Your Divorce, p111, Companion Press).*

"Keep the strife out of your life by learning how to relate to the other person..."

If you are going through difficulty in your marriage, do not just give up in frustration. Too many couples have given up at that stage; the negative thinking of one or both husband and wife took down their marriage. One should never cherish negative expectations but positive ideas in believing that they will succeed.

Avoid Arguments

In your early years of marriage, you would have the urge to foster a good argument and tell the other what you think and how you feel things should be done. But that is not the way God wants you to live. That is not His best for you. If you listen to His still, small voice deep down, it is saying to you, "let it go, you are better than that; quit living on such low levels."

Make a decision not to want to prove that you are right, but what is best to say would keep peace in your home. Those positive thoughts will help you relinquish the fighting traits that plague you and be an easy going husband or wife. Let it become part of your character and take you to a higher level of worth. When either one opens their mouth to reprove the other, your intention should be well thought out that you appeal to their common sense and conscience. *(CS Lewis, Surprised by Joy The Shape of My Early Life, Harcourt Brace & Company; p. 38).*

Swim Through The Conflict

While you are single, accessible, and disengaged, your troubles are different from what is experienced within a marriage relationship. Marriage life can be likened to the ocean. At times it has little wind moving the waters. There is no wind whatsoever, and the water is so still as if one can lie on it, while at times the water is exceptionally active, that even the most experienced captain is afraid to sail his ship on it.

Always maintain your calm; this will help you to pull back from conflict. The ocean of marriage emotions will become turbulent, and you may feel you are drowning while the other seems to be staying afloat comfortably. Use Christ's techniques: do not look down at the waves churning beneath your feet. You will lose your faith and begin to sink. Use biblical principles and values. Christ will take the matter in hand, and you will learn to swim through the turbulence *(see Matthew 14:22-33)*.

Teeth And Tongue Will Knock

When the brain is not in gear and the head is not with the heart, what began as a simple matter results in an uncontrollable fire (Author Unknown). This wildfire will destroy the marriage if the teeth and tongue keep the marriage warm and comfortable.

"Teeth and tongue will knock," but if you are not nagging, your heads and hearts will keep the knocking soothing to the ears.

Paul advised, "Be angry and sin not; let not the sun go down upon your wrath" *(Ephesians 4:26)*. Angry moments are experienced when one's mind is in chartered waters, and the other's mind is not sharing that sphere as yet. Common sense makes the difference at this moment.

It Is Not Always About Being Right

A couple who were both my friends lived together for about six years before they finally got married. During their life together, there was conflict after conflict, and most times, these conflicts were not resolved.

I was amazed when the male partner told me that they would get married and wanted me to be the Master of Ceremonies of the second phase of the celebrations. I was glad for them and requested that they seek counsel before embarking upon that more profound commitment. Unfortunately, they did not take my advice.

At the wedding reception, everything went awry. At an appropriate time, I called him aside and asked him why things were so disorganized. His remark was, "Next time, things would be better." I cannot tell if the celebrations got to his head hence his statement, but sure enough, there was the next time. The marriage lasted nine (9) days!

I can still recall being called to the home because of a conflict, the young lady had left and I saw the beautifully decorated cake still sitting on the dining table. Only the indentation of the sharing piece was missing.

There was another time for celebration because both the young lady and young man are re-married. I do not know how those celebrations went and how the marriages are going. I cannot tell since they are both still living in the United States of America.

Kiss And Make Up Right Away

Apologize first. It is fair, for it will keep you together. Swallow your pride; be the bigger person and sow the seed of love and God will make it up to you.

Be a peacemaker. Live in peace in your home, after all you are God's instrument. Be the first to respond and the Holy Spirit will keep life in the marriage. He will allow sensitivity of one another to prevail. *(Tom Smail, The Giving Gift: The Holy Spirit in Person, London: Dorton,*

Longman and Todd, 1994; p. 175). Do not wait until you cannot make amends with your spouse. Do it today. Swallow your pride even if it was not your fault. It is not about always being right; it is about keeping strife out of your life.

Do not try to win every argument. It opens the door to turmoil, and tears you asunder; in the end you lose a lot. So when you are tempted to be argumentative, fault-finding, a recorder of all wrongs, listen to God's still soft voice calling upon you to be the peace maker.

Put A Noose Around Your Tongue

"Paying back wrong for wrong is unscriptural."

It is said that before you lose your patience, you should "bite your tongue" or "swallow your spittle ten times." There is much wisdom in those words and James advises that, *"the tongue is a fire, a world of iniquity; so is the tongue among our members that it defileth the whole body and setteth on fire the course of nature and it is set on fire of hell. Even so, the tongue is a little member and boasteth great things. Behold how great a matter a little fire kindleth"* (James 3:5-6).

Constantly harping on your wife or your husband, criticizing and correcting everything they do, and questioning every decision made will cause the earth beneath your feet to lose its hardness and soon enough cause you to sink in oblivion. Sometimes it is better to bite your tongue or swallow your saliva so long as the situation does not get out of hand. We are reminded *"the more talk, the less truth; the wise measure their words"* (Prov. 10:19).

Consider Your Partner Better Than Yourself

There is a caution, *"Do nothing out of selfish ambition or vain conceit, but in humility consider others better than yourselves."* Each of you should look not only to your interests but also to the interests of others *(Phil. 2:3-4)*. The practice *"Christ first, others next, self last"* should be applied in every marriage relationship *(Carolyn Larsen, China)*.

If this practice is adopted as the motto for marriage partners and taken as the number one priority, there is no way the marriage will go under or find itself between a rock and a hard place. The union will stand on the rock of its life.

John, in his Gospel, gives us a flash-back to Jesus' direction to lay down your life for a friend – that is real love. Serving each other to fulfill individual goals and objectives should be very important to the other.

The Hymn writer has aptly put in lyrics from his thoughts when he records:

> *Love is kind and suffers long*
> *Love is meek and thinks no wrong*
> *Love than death itself more strong*
> *Therefore give us love*
> *(A&M Hymnal 210)*

You Will Never Know All About Each Other

Indeed, you will never know one another entirely as our Lord knows us (Achtenmeier p134). Do believe it, you do not know everything about all subjects in the world, neither will you know all about your partner. Every day you will learn something new, and even after fifty years together, you will still be learning about each other. There will be stimulating discussions, sharing of viewpoints, and challenging observations involved in the learning and growing process. So appreciate what you can both do for each other.

A knife can never sharpen itself; it takes another instrument to point it. Therefore sharpen each other with gentleness, kind attitudes, and loving words. You will be richer for the way ahead.

God's Love Is Unfailing

"Many are the woes of the wicked, but the Lord's unfailing love surrounds the man who trusts in Him" (Psalm 32:10).

Can that statement be coined better?. It is called unconditional love. It never fails. Put anchor down here; it is perfect. Human love can be good, robust, compelling, but not perfect. This love sometimes disappoints, breaks the heart, and breaks trust. God's love in Christ is unfailing. It stays around you unconditionally without any failure.

Be honest with God; tell Him everything. Nothing will make Him quiver or quake. Christ's love is constant. It is always in the present tense. Hold on to this love; trust it always.

Love Knows No End

It is incredible to know that love has no end. The apostle Paul says, *"Love never fails" (1 Cor. 13:8).*

He admonishes that everything else in life fails—the things of life rot, decay, and fade. Friends die, loved ones pass away, careers come to an end, but love stays forever - count on it.

God's love is forever; it is constant and never disappoints. When all was said and done, it was love that was left standing at the Cross of Calvary, *"Father forgive them for they know not what they do" (Luke 23:34).*

If you let God's love guide you, it will assist you in your relationship with your spouse. It will be an "unfailing" and "unforgiving" love. That love puts the other's needs first. It is not a stubborn love - it will never fail.

Hold Not On To One's Wrong

Be careful not to hold on to a wrong word or a wrong action of others - especially in the marriage. You will never fulfill your duty as a husband or a wife with that kind of attitude.

"To expect perfection is extremely unfair and places much pressure on the other individual."

There is a story of the husband who was unfaithful to his wife. He asked for forgiveness, but she held on to the wrong for some time.

73

Every time they sat at the dinner table, she would wear a particular scarf to remind him of his past unfaithfulness.

Such actions lead to evil. Therefore, the scripture says to forgive and forget. When God forgives, that matter is buried. He has forgotten it. Husband and wife are to leave all shortcomings behind.

We are told *"to refrain from anger and turn from wrath,"* fueling leads to evil *(Psalm 37:8 NIV)*.

Jesus Has The Spirit And Counsel Of God

The prophet Isaiah directs anyone who trusts in God that *"the spirit of the Lord will rest on Him the spirit of wisdom and understanding - the spirit of counsel and power, the spirit of knowledge and fear of the Lord - and He will delight in fear of the Lord"* (Is. 11:2-3).

Isaiah tells us in these few words a lot about God and hence calls for absolute trust in His son Jesus Christ. Jesus can counsel and direct lives. He stands in the house, alert to handle whatever life throws at His children. So as long as He is in the place, all will be well.

The three Hebrew boys were thrown into the furnace when they placed their lives on the line through their faith *(see Daniel 3:1-18)*. Daniel chose honesty and was thrown into the lion's den to be crushed by the hungry lions *(see Daniel 5:16)*.

Daniel and the three Hebrew boys were fully aware that God was in the house. They placed all confidence in His being. Examine their faith, *"If we are thrown in the blazing furnace, the God we serve can save us…and He will rescue us from your hands, O King. But even if He does not, we are confident…that we will not serve your God and worship your image of gold (Daniel 3:17-18)*. God who put you in the house will assist you in the place. Take a stand and suffer the consequences.

Be Mature

It takes maturity to get along with somebody different from you.

Maturity makes one very comfortable with openness, to be able to see someone else's viewpoint or new path filled with hope and potential. *(Stephen Arterburn, Walking Into Walls. 5 Blind Spots That Block God's work in You; Worthy publishing, p. 13).*

A mature person does not become easily offended over minor issues. A marriage relationship is "bankrupt without maturity." Keep strife out of your life and learn how to relate to the other. Always give that person the benefit of the doubt. No one is perfect—not even the person with whom you are in a relationship. The person may be great and loving; however, you will become offended with some things that that person said or did. Remember, there is no such thing as a perfect boss, spouse, father, mother, sibling, or Pastor.

It was mentioned earlier that love is not a feeling but a choice, a commitment. With these attributes, you will never find yourself saying, "he irritates me," "I can not stand her being around me anymore," "why is she trying so hard to be with me?" or "I do not feel in love with him anymore."

Your marriage relationship is not like a two-lane tunnel. Try your best not to exit your lane. Your love life is a one-lane highway. Drive with understanding; when one becomes upset, there is no other lane on which to turn.

commitment. With these attributes you will never find yourself saying, "he irritates me," "I can not stand her being around me anymore," "why is she trying so hard to be with me?" or "I do not feel in love with him anymore."

Your marriage relationship is not like a two lane tunnel. Try your best not to exit your lane. Your love life is a one lane highway. Drive with understanding; when one becomes upset there is no other lane on which to turn.

Say The Word

If you want peace, if you're going to feel close to your spouse, if you're going to be understood, if you're going to experience a healthy marriage the way God intends, tell your spouse that you love and highly respect them. Do not feel awkward saying these words. You told them at the beginning when you wanted them to go out with you on a date. You will be surprised at the positive reaction.

Every time words of admiration are said to your spouse, her demeanor will become more positive in an instant. Do not forget to say, "I love that dress you are wearing, 'Babe, that hairstyle makes you beautiful,' 'I love it when you open the door for me Tom;' or you elate me when you say such nice things to me."

HAVE A CLEAR VISION

Do Not Be An Authority On Everything

In your conversations, give your spouse an equal chance to speak and react. "Do not be a "know it all." They who knows it all perfect. Only one is perfect - Christ Jesus. Do not always "hog" first place. Those who always have to have the last say are difficulty living together. Love— true love corrects this attitude.

Encourage the other to share their openness. It will lift your marriage to higher heights. Listen to the other's opinions and do not insist that your way is always right, or worse yet, belittle the other's idea and comment.

"Nothing can happen to you that is not in His providence."

Look for ways to help your spouse feel intelligent and valuable. Love will build up your partner. This enables your spouse to gain confidence and grow in wisdom. Each of you and your marriage will benefit from living in love.

Keep Your Motives Pure

Be dependable. Keep your motives pure. Be obedient to each other and grow in your service one to another. Do not be selfish. Do not waver in your support of each other. Your goal should be to look out for each other constantly. Seek each other for guidance, encouragement, and strength.

"Throughout your life, God has used others to influence your life for good to follow His will to seek His kingdom and to know His heart. You influence others by following Him yourself" (Roy Lessin). "Lord, how oft shall my brothers sin against me and I forgive him, seven times? Not until seven times, but until seventy times seven" (Matthew 18:21-22 KJV).

Be Humble

Our example of humility is perfected in our Saviour, Jesus Christ. He left the glory of heaven and came to earth as a servant, *"not to be ministered unto but to minister"* *(Matt 20:28)*. This was His way of showing what it means to put the needs of others before one's own.

Living in humility is an act of love. It demonstrates genuine empathy for others around you. Emulate Christ's example in your marriage by clothing yourself in humility. God can help you rid yourself of what is not of such a qualified state and fill your heart with what it takes to be humble.

Christians are advised to clothe themselves with humility toward one another because *"God opposes the proud but gives grace to the humble" (see 1 Peter 5:5).*

Be Understanding

Sometimes you will discover that the other half does not know what you are going through. One may explain with all might, and the other would not be on the same wavelength.

It makes sense to wait on God for the other half to come on board. To rush the brush is to get wiped with the wrong color paint. Patience comes in. To do otherwise spells disaster.

Do not lose your cool; God never lost His with you; have an understanding heart. You are special. Jesus never lost His cool when the two thieves were ridiculing Him; as such, one of the thieves found salvation just before he died *(see Matthew 27:44; Luke 23;40-43-43).*

Do Not Play A Pay Back Game

Paying back wrong for wrong is unscriptural. "Carol did not answer my questions, so I stayed out with the boys." "He did not help with the children, so I withheld sex for a month." "She did not iron my shirts for work, so I did not put my part of our house allowance." "We are not on terms because she made some unkind remarks."

When your marriage is in a state of "If you do not do this then, I will not do that," it is on a downward spiral. Payback kills relationships. If pay-back resides at your door, kill it immediately. It shows up to do grievous marriage harm.

Please talk with your spouse about their attitude. This is the right direction for the relationship. Sometimes, the accused is not even aware of the wrong that triggered the payback.

Christians are reminded that they make sure that there is no payback among them. They are always to be kind to each other and to everyone else. Do not pay back wrong for wrong *(1 Thess. 5:15).*

Let Christ Stabilize You

All gymnasts who fix their eyes on an object claim that that is their stabilizer. Some stand on a slender object suspended in the air and spin around without falling off. Some jump, flip, dance on beams, and do not get dizzy. While others do two or more rotations, just simply focusing on one steady focal point. "Plow with your eye on the fence post...by staying focused on a point across the field, a person plowing is assured of a straight line." *(Randy Kilgore, Plowing Strait Lines. Our Daily Bread, November 7, 2011).*

The rotation is connected depending on how many times one passed his focal point. This is a simple lesson of trust. The couple who fix their eyes on Christ finds Him as their stabilizer no matter what else is happening in their lives.

The apostle Peter focused on Jesus as his stabilizer. As Peter fixed his eyes he made strides on the water as a footpath. It was when Peter lost trust, hope, and confidence—simply put, when Peter doubted, that he began to sink.

Jesus took care of His people time after time. He did so even when those people did not obey Him. Remember where you were over the years! Look at where you are now; who brought you here? I am sure you can recall when you did not go Christ's way, yet His care for you is evident.

God is trustworthy. Once your eyes are fixed on Him, none can change or overshadow the relationship.

Your Relationship With God Counts

No one places confidence in someone he does not know. As one comes to know God and his relationship grows, there is a world of difference for life ahead.

How would the relationship grow? Would the walk have meaning? Such confidence is derived from reading daily the Word of God. God speaks through His Word. There is scripture He reveals His character, His love, His direction, and His desired obedience.

The songwriter says, "Take time out for Jesus He took time for you" *(Charley Pride 1971)*. If you want Christ to spend time with you, you have to spend time with Him in prayer, meditation, and in His word. In this manner, you will understand His love which He declares, passes all human comprehension.

Serve Each Other

"As you go head to head and solve the problem, you become heart to heart" (Eggerich p. 187). For whom are you living to please? In the marriage, you are living to please each other. Assisting the other determines the choices you make and the path you follow.

The priorities in your life have much to do with the needs of both husband and wife. Pleasing them becomes the essential thing in life. This is what you agreed to at the very beginning of your new venture. I, John, will agree to assist Mary to fulfill her dreams and aspirations. The reciprocation is also proper.

To serve each other as you walk in the marriage, you need to listen to the Holy Spirit. The Holy Spirit will show you how to listen to each other, respect each other's point of view, say no, when to say yes, and apologize *(Dr. Henry Claud & John Townsend, How People Grow, Zondervan, 2001 p. 94-95).*

Serve God In Whatever You Do

Solomon advises all that, *"Whatever your hands find to do, do it with all your will" (Eccles. 9:10).* He refers to actions that are possible. We sometimes want to do many things, but they are not possible. This should not bother us. What should be uppermost in our minds is to be effective servants of Christ, not talking about our schemes, but be practical and carry out whatever our hands find to do.

One cannot be effective in theories and great opportunities. God effectively makes the reality of the brilliant view and uses every opportunity daily to achieve his goals.

Do not wait for the right opportunity to please the other, do it now. Do not put off pleasing God for tomorrow; please Him now. There is no way you can please God by doing what He requires tomorrow. Do for God Today. Do for each other today.

Our lot is a gift from God. We are reminded that we enjoy what we worked for when God gives us wealth, possessions, health, and strength. That is what God requires *(Eccles. 5:19-20).*

Has God blessed you with your gifts - wealth, health, and a career? Are you happy with it? Do you want to change it for that of another's? Do not daydream anymore. Do not allow your heart to be occupied with the wrong things.

Focus your heart on thanking God for what He has done and the blessings He has provided, and press on to work.

In the past, you have been looking at the glass half empty. If you focus and stay focused, you will see the way forward being magnified, and a positive attitude will be aroused for you to see the glass half full.

Negative vibes breed damaging muscles and what has been an easy walk over time becomes serious and insurmountable. God will lift the burden that holds you down. The Psalmist gives his assurance, *"O God, you are my fortress, my loving God" (Psalm 59:17).*

Do Not Love Expecting Not To Be Hurt

The attitude: "I will love you as long as you never hurt me" will never take effect. The person who makes mistakes will do things that will upset you. Even your friends sometimes do not treat you right. So no one is perfect. To expect perfection is extraordinarily unfair and places much pressure on the other individual. Love makes provision for human weaknesses. Love covers a person's faults. Be prepared to overlook some things.

Do not demand perfection from your spouse, children, or others who are in the relationship. Learn to exercise the Lord's mercy.

To you, it may not seem like someone has a perfect life, but maybe they are as happy as can be. Or you might see someone who looks like they do not worry about the world, but they are dying of pain; it just de-pends on the person and how you look at it. Maybe someone doesn't have a car and has to bike to work. Perhaps they don't have a TV and have to learn how to entertain themselves. Maybe they have a small house and a low-paying job. But maybe that person is happy with what they do have and do not need anymore. Perhaps life is simply the way they want it, and life is excellent and perfect for them. Then, on the other hand, you may see a person that lives in a mansion, has a pool, is one of the wealthiest people you know, which seems perfect, but maybe they want even more and can still manage to find flaws or perhaps they have other problems which you cannot see. Yes, there are people in the world that have a per-fect life according to them or the people around them. It all depends on what perfect means to you (Metal Fox, Is there any in the world who has a perfect life *(http://www. Google.com)*.

Find The Beauty In The Other Person

Finding the beauty in the other person enables you to appreciate how ex-tremely loving, caring, and generous that person is. But remember, there will be some things you will have to overlook. You will have to make allowance for other things simply because that person is just human. Be-ing a fault finder, keeping account of wrongs your spouse does to you, will result in the relationship becoming sour, and before you know it, there is a war in the relationship.

A wise man once said, "Love though natural and spontaneous in its origin, must not be regarded as a thing to be left to itself. Constant thought and care are indispensable to its higher perfection and beauty."

Make your demeanor one of graciousness. Do not force yourself upon your spouse. Always seek the best for them while respecting their inner qualities. *(Matthew Barnett with George Barna. The Cause within you: Finding the one great thing you were created to do in this world; Library of Congress Cataloging-in-Publication Data. P 97)*.

Make space for weaknesses, and do not be easily offended. Do not be touchy or over-sensitive. Shake off the offense and use it as a stepping stone to the next level—Loo for the best in each other.

Your Vote Is Important

God had willed your marriage to work when He took His place in it. And He formed the three-legged relationship. He has voted success for the union. Your vote in the relationship is essential. If your casting vote is a daunting image in the marriage, you have decided to do your best to crush the ex-traordinary life you are destined to share.

Sometimes the bottom of your married life is bursting to fall out, but if your attitude is God's, He will push back what has been falling and seal the entire bottom so that your continued life will be better than before. You will barely make it; you will positively make it.

Vote this way: Both hands are tightly clasped, and the other hands hold on to God *(Getting Married, Family Doctor Publication. Published by British Medical Association. 1977. p. 40).*

Believe For The Best

One writer said that we become what we believe. Therefore believe that you will move higher and higher each day away from your obstacles. Believe each day you will live in God's abundant supply, health, healing, and victo-ry.

Be proud of who you are day by day, for you will be who you are because of what you believed yesterday and will be tomorrow what you think today.

God sees you as a conqueror, one who is working with Him to succeed. He sees you as ahead and not a tail, as being a victor and not a victim. God sees you as one who will rise to new levels of fulfilment. So God says the decision is yours, and it will be done to you accordingly. "Become what you believe."

SEEKING GOD IN YOUR MARRIAGE
♥ ♥ ♥

God's Compassion Is Forever

Rub off your knees before Him. When you are full of regrets and guilt and do not even want to see God, you need to fix your faith and confidence in Him.

Over and over, you ask for forgiveness for the sins you have commit-ted, and He forgives you. You have promised never to engage them again, and there you are, asking for forgiveness again because He loves you, and as far as He is concerned, every day means a second chance for His children. This second chance is based simply on His compassion which is renewed every day.

Since God loves you so much, you can certainly trust Him to stay over you every day. The Hymn writer states, "He will take care of you! God will take care of you." Lamentation advises, "Because of the Lord's great love we are not consumed, for His compassions never fail, they are re-newed every morning; great is your faithfulness *(Lam. 3:22-23).*

Fear of the world, when at your doorstep, traps keep you as a slave. The safest place in all the world is God. He protects you unconditionally. He wants no bodyguard. The psalmist reminds, *"When I am afraid, I will trust in you."* In God, you have no fear. He can be trusted while mortals cannot *(Psalm 56:3-4).*

Afraid? Trust God to protect and care for you. Nothing can happen to you that is not in His providence. God always knows what is next in your life.

Lord May, I Do Your Will?

When informed of God's choice of her to be the mother of His son Jesus Christ, the teenager Mary readily gave in to His request. I am the Lord's servant, "… *may it be to me as you wish" (Luke 1:38).*

Mary did not bother to think of the gossip corners: I am not married, so what will others think of me. She paid no consideration to the consequences within her society, friend, and family.

This was an incredible trust in Mary's response to the messenger God's angel. *"Whatever God wants is fine with me. My life is His fu-ture, and I trust Him with it."*

Your married life should be considered in this term. *"Okay, God, do whatever you want with this marriage, say it and mean it. You may not see how this may logically work out for your good, trust Him anyway. He will do it."*

We are reminded that the pudding taste is in the eating, so taste and trust Christ on the way. He is having God as your friend means fearing Him. His power is incredible, and He has a fit of jealousy for the love you have for Him. He demands attention and accountability for what or who reigns in our hearts.

Fearing God is fantastic; it requires giving Him the respect He deserves. Be in awe of Him, recognize His power, for it is in such status that we are given all we need.

The Psalmist reminds us to *"taste and see that the Lord is good and only those who take refuge in Him are blessed, and those who fear Him lack nothing" (Psalm 34:8-9).*

You and your marriage are part of a plan. God's faithfulness will continue; His purpose laid out long ago. The more you grow in His strength and power, the more His goal will be worked out in you.

God's Blessings Knows No End

God's blessing begins with His call. Abraham and Sarah experienced it, and so did Isaac and Rebekah. You will never live one second with-out God's enabling grace.

Moses coined it nicely for you, *"The Lord Jesus bless you and keep you; the Lord make His face shine upon you and be gracious to you; the Lord turn His face toward you and give you peace" (Numbers 6:24-26).*

God's blessings call for a response in your life. You have to walk towards Him at all times. His peace lies in the very path you are traveling. God's face turns towards you, so He sees any chaos that is creeping up along the way.

The excellent assurance you have in all this confidence is that God's place does not change. Do not move your focus away from Him. God's peace is forever.

Blessings In Disguise

As followers of Christ, you need to know that problems sometimes have a purpose. Nobody rejoices over their difficulties; God does not expect merriment either. What He does expect is that we will triumph over the result of the problem.

Amid problems, it is challenging to stay connected to God, but staying close to Him in the walk produces health, strength, faith, and peace, which only He can give. Making it through difficult times helps more couples know that they can get through the others one at a time.

Problems in disguise need perseverance which helps faith to grow and builds confidence, no matter the outcome. Do you know what is ahead? Go with Him. It is a blessing in disguise.

No Tug-of-War With God

You and your spouse may play the tug-of-war game to see who will win, but do not play the tug-of-war game with God. Tug-of-war is a struggle of strength and will. Struggling with God means that you want to have your way in life. If you do this, you stand to lose.

Trust God and do good; dwell in His land and enjoy safe pasture. If you and your spouse delight in the Lord, He will give you the desires of your heart. (see Psalm 37:3-4).

Make your will for your marriage to be aligned with His. In this way, the struggles that your marriage experiences will have their foundation in Him. As your wedding grows with God each day and your relationship with God and each other deepens, your service to God will be more successful.

Be Silent Before God

So much energy is spent worrying about what might happen around the corner. Chores and worries pile up every day to create burdens. Matthew advises, *"Not to worry about tomorrow as tomorrow will have its worries. Each day has its trouble"* (Matthew 6:34).

Use each day to be silent before God. Search His Word and listen for the still small voice. God will speak and give the money to make it through each journey. Stay focused; do not worry about the future; take life one day at a time.

Let Your Mind Stay On Him

Problems may have rippled through your marriage and done such incredi-ble damage that your faith is diminished, and your only option is to lift your hands towards heaven in awe! When situations like this confront you, look to the center of your chaos, and there is where you will find the peace that only God can give to keep you calm.

What a fantastic assurance of hope. Jesus is standing in the dark and scary moments, saying, "peace be still." If the eye of a hurricane can be so calm, God can and will do it for you and your partner.

Amid your anxiety, stress, and dark moments of your marriage, focus your mind on God and leave it there, for He promises to give you peace in the center of the storm.

Nothing Is Too Hard For God

If God made the heaven and the earth by His great power and with His outstretched arms, be assured that nothing is too hard for Him to do for you once it is His will *(see Jeremiah 32:17)*.

God made everything on earth and in heaven for you. He controls them too; from the delicate flower to the mighty volcano, he manages the man-eating shark, thunderstorms, sunsets, and you from the birds to the vast oceans.

Use your free will on this earth to hand over to Him your marriage, and let His control guide your conscience. Remember God made your mind, so he knows how complete your thoughts are, determining your decision-making process. Nothing is too hard for Him.

The way you live shows what your life reflects on God. No Christian words, prayers, tithe, reading of His Word say how good God is. Your trust, honesty, treatment of others, the management of your time, talent, treasure, and talent speaks volumes of God to others.

Christians who have and practice a Christ-like attitude, who hold firm to their faith in Christ, who do not live for the praise of man but do God's will by following Christ's example show who the God of the universe is. Remember Christ says, *"He who sees me sees the father, they see Him because of the work I do" (John 14:11)*. Do not depend on external things or persons to see you through life. Those who do such or look for such security are doomed. No person's wealth or other material worth can give you value; that is a sad mistake—none of those can provide you complete salvation.

All persons are equal in the sight of God. Therefore, respect others and respect yourselves. Respect a person because they are God's child. When life is placed in God's hands, the Christian will thrive and grow like a healthy plant.

Focus On God

When you focus on God, you will stay resolute even with harmful elements in your life. You will not focus on what you are not, what you do not have or what you cannot do, but you will look steadfast on your possibilities, and your faith will cause God to work supernaturally in your life.

The faith of the husband or wife or both will change obstacles and reach new victory levels. So have the right outlook! Do not focus on your prob-lems; focus on God!

The faith of countless persons in Holy Scripture caused Jesus' compassion to flow to their relief. His response was, "According to your faith be it done unto you" (Matt 20:30-34).

Suggestions for Further Reading

Denton, Wallace. *Family problems and what to do about them*. The Westminister Press, 1971

Chesser Eustace. *Love Without Fear.* New York 1949

Fr Chuck Gallagher. *The Marriage Encounter : As I Have Loved You.* New York 1975

REFERENCES

Cloud, Henry. *Changes That Heal, How To Understand Your Past To Ensure A Healthier Future,* Zondervan 1992.

Graham Lotz, Anne. The Magnificent Obsession: *Embracing the God-filled Life.* Zondervan 2009

McCullough, Jackie. *Satisfaction of the Soul.* USA: Destiny Image Publishers, Inc, 1987.

Osteen, Joel. *Your Best Life Now—7 Steps to Living at your full Potential.* New York: ner Faith, 2004.

Cymbaca, Carol. *Trusting God to do What Only He can do.* Zondervan, 2001.

Book of Common Prayer of the Province of West Indies. Collect for Sunday, Proper 28, page 181.

Cloud, Henry and John Townsend. *Rescue Your Love Life: Change Those Dumb Attitudes and Behaviours That Will Sink Your Marriage.* Thomas Nelson, 2005.

Pitt, Theodore K. *Premarital Counseling Handbook for Ministers.* Judson Press Val-ley Forge, 1985

Thomas and Thomas. *Beginning Your Marriage, 8th Edition.* Illinois: ACTA Publica-tions, 1994.

Eggerichs, Emerson. *Love & Respect.* Thomas Nelson, 2004.

Shakespeare, William. *The Tragedy of Hamlet Prince of Denmark.* Vol. XLVI, Part 2. The Harvard Classics. New York: P.F. Collier & Son, 1909–14; Bartleby.com, 2001.

It Only Take A Spark. Song by Texan Baptist Church Choir, 1969

Copeland, Gloria. *God's Master Plan for your life. Keys to fulfilling your Destiny.* Berkley Publication Group, 2007.
Femenia, Nora. *Five Tips to Time Proof your Marriage, Participant's Guide, 2nd Edi-tion.* Outreach Publication, 2008.

Achtenmeier, Elizabeth. *The Committee Marriage,* Westminster Press, 1976.

Getting Married. Family Doctor Publication. British Medical Association. 1977.

The Book of Common Prayer, The Church in the Province of the West Indies, 1995.

Cloud, Henry. *The Law of Happiness.* Howards Books, 2011.

Edmeade, James. *Before Your Divorce.* Companion Press, 1994.

Lessin, Roy. *His Footsteps, My Pathway.* Christian Art Gift, RSA, 2007.

Smith, Martin, L. Reconciliation for Confession in the Episcopal Church..

Turner, Phillip. *Sex Money and Power.* Massachusetts: Cowley Publications, 1985

Rossie, Dick BD DD Litt. *Premarital Guidance,* New Jersey: Englewood, Cliff, 1963.

McKnight, Scot. *From Wheaton To Rome: Evangelicals Become Roman Catholic Journal of the Evangelical theological Society.* Volume: JETS 45/3, 2002.

Feiler, Bruce. *Abraham.* Harper College publishers, 2004.

Larsen, One Minute Devotions for Women, May 17

Yancey, Philip D. Where Is God When It Hurts? 1977, Zondervan

Dicks, Russell. *Premarital Guidance.* Prentice-Hall 1963.

Zahnd, Brian. *Unconditional? Florida:* Charisma House A Strand Company, 2010

Clinebell, Howard. *Basic types of Pastoral Care Counselling. Resources for the Ministry of Healing and Growth, [Revised and enlarged]* Abingdon Press, 1984.

The Message, The Bible in Contemporary Language, Numbered Edition; Luke 11:17

White Ellen G. Adventist Home,

Lewis, C. S. *Surprised by Joy The shape of My Early Life.* Harcourt Brace & Compa-ny.

Smail, Tom. *The Giving Gift: The Holy Spirit in Person,* London: Dorton, Longman and Todd, 1994.

Arterburn, Stephen. *Walking Into Walls. 5 Blind Spots That Block God's work in You.* Worthy publishing, 1984.

Pride, Charley, "Take time out for Jesus He took time for You." 1971

Cloud, Henry, and John Townsend, *How People Grow.* Zondervan, 2001 Barnett, Matthew and George Barna. *The Cause within you: Finding the one great thing you were created to do in this world.* Library of Congress Cataloging-in-Publication Data.

Fox, Metal. *Is there any in the world who has a perfect life* http://www. google.com

PREVIEW

Two-Shall-Be-One, is a brilliant, all-inclusive well written and clinical synopsis of the institution of marriage, by Reverend Dr. Alson B H Percival. Calling upon his discipline as a priest, he combines his training as a theologian with his hands on experience as a Spiritual Counsellor, to produce a very comprehensive manual for a happy, lasting, God-inspired and God- led marriage.

Notwithstanding the theme throughout of a marriage relationship between two individuals destined to live together as one, that is to say, one in hope, one in planning, one in embracing a successful and harmonious conjugal relationship, of a union based on faith and dependent upon the inspiration of God's indwelling Holy Spirit, the book nevertheless would prove to be an indispensable manual for any married couple, to have and enjoy a fully healthy and lasting life together as a union.

The author's academic and intellectual expertise are displayed throughout; but the book is written for an easy read for any person who is desirous of learning how to forge a successful marriage relationship. But also, in the view of this writer, would constitute a very practical teaching tool.

All in all, the book is a must read for anyone who has an interest in the institution of marriage in general, and the various components which are necessary when considering the essential characteristics of a happy, lasting and fruitful marriage, in particular. For even if one were to strip this work entirely of its spiritual elements, it would still be rich in nuggets of practical wisdom, advice and counselling, in every undertaking involving a successful, and fruitful partnership between spouses.

Preview
By
Rev. John S Weekes. B. A. Law, TH. D, Rel. Ed. D
Author.

SUMMARY

I have known the Venerable Dr. B. A. Percival for several decades having been a parishioner and a Lay Reader in his first major pastoral assignment in St. Peter's Parish in Montserrat, West Indies and remained in close contact with him over the years as he continued his ministry across the Diocese of the North Eastern Caribbean and Aruba and further afield. His Tips and wide ranging advice to clients are easy to comprehend and apply in practice. They are all based on unchanging Biblical principles of love and mutual respect among participants. Undoubtedly, this book by the Venerable Dr. B. A. Percival is a significant contribution to the field of pastoral counseling'.

Submitted by Joseph W. (Jim) Bass M. Sc (Econ).

Printed in the United States
by Baker & Taylor Publisher Services